Wars in Peace
and the Cold War

The
MILITARY HISTORY
of the
UNITED STATES

Christopher Chant

WARS IN PEACE
AND THE COLD WAR

MARSHALL CAVENDISH
NEW YORK · LONDON · TORONTO · SYDNEY

Library Edition Published 1992

© Marshall Cavendish Limited 1992

Published by
Marshall Cavendish Corporation
2415 Jerusalem Avenue
PO Box 587
North Bellmore
New York 11710

Series created by Graham Beehag Book Design

Series Editor	Maggi McCormick
Consultant Editors	James R. Arnold
	Roberta Wiener
Sub Editor	Julie Cairns
Designer	Graham Beehag
Illustrators	John Batchelor
	Steve Lucas
	Terry Forest
	Colette Brownrigg
Indexer	Mark Dartford

The publishers wish to thank the following organizations who have supplied photographs:

The National Archives, Washington. United States Navy, United States Marines, United States Army, United States Air Force, Department of Defense, Library of Congress, The Smithsonian Institution.

The publishers gratefully thank the U.S. Army Military History Institute, Carlisle Barracks, PA. for the use of archive material for the following witness accounts:

Page 57
Report of Stability Operations in the Dominican Republic U.S. Army, 1965

Page 83
From Message P270342Z Oct. '83 ZN, Operation Urgent Fury, Grenada.

Page 100
U.S. Marines in Lebanon, 1982-1984 by Benis M. Frank (U.S. Government Printing Office).

Library of Congress Cataloging-in-Publication Data

Chant, Christopher.
 The Military History of the United States / Christopher Chant –
Library ed.
  p. cm.
 Includes bibliographical references and index.
 Summary: Surveys the wars that have directly influenced the
 United States., from the Revolutionary War through the Cold War.
 ISBN 1-85435-365-90 ISBN 1-85435-361-9 (set)
  1. United States - History, Military - Juvenile literature.
 [1. United States - History, Military.] I. Title.
 t181.C52 1991
 973 - dc20   90 - 19547
                                                 CIP
                                                 AC

Printed in Singapore by Times Offset PTE Ltd
Bound in the United States

Contents

Between the end of World War II in 1945 and the beginning of the "Desert Storm" conflict with Iraq in 1990, the military events that effected the American people most drastically were the Korean War (1950-1953) and the Vietnam War (1962-1973). Yet they were not the only conflicts involving American forces during this period, and although these other episodes were too small to be called wars, they were still important in American history.

The Berlin Airlift
(1948)

At the end of World War II, defeated Germany had been divided into four zones occupied by the Allies. Of these, the eastern zone was the Soviet area of responsibility, while the three western zones were occupied by the British in the north, the Americans in the south, and the French as two pockets in the southwest. Berlin, Germany's capital, lay deep in the Soviet zone, but it too was divided into American, British, French, and Soviet zones like the rest of the country. The inter-Allied agreement governing the German's division into zones of occupation made provision for the Western Allies to have rights of communication with their zones in the western half of Berlin via road, rail, water, and air routes.

During World War II, there had been a move in the United States for the postwar deindustrialization of Germany, thereby removing any possibility that Germany might start a third world war to follow the two world wars it had already started. The British and the French command opposed any such thought and believed that the best way

The major effort in the Berlin airlift was made by the transport aircraft of the U.S. Air Force, with support from the British Royal Air Force. Another important contribution came from civilian operators with aircraft such as these British Avro Lancastrian transports.

The Berlin Airlift.

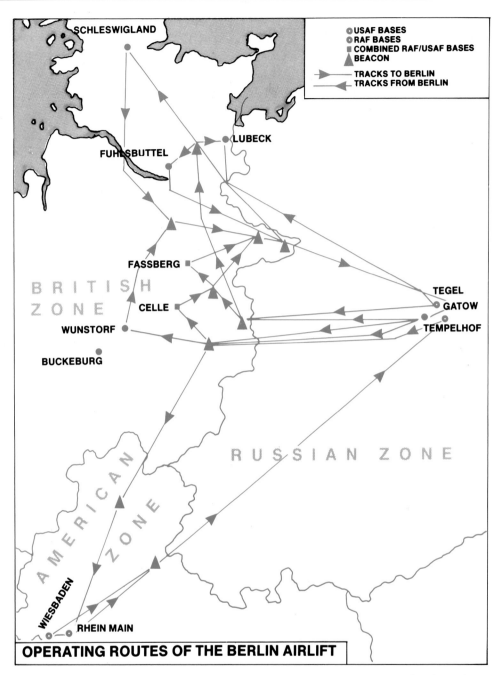

Legend:
- ⊙ USAF BASES
- ⊙ RAF BASES
- ■ COMBINED RAF/USAF BASES
- ▲ BEACON
- → TRACKS TO BERLIN
- ← TRACKS FROM BERLIN

SCHLESWIGLAND

LUBECK

FUHLSBUTTEL

FASSBERG ■

B R I T I S H
Z O N E

CELLE ■

TEGEL
GATOW
TEMPELHOF

WUNSTORF

BUCKEBURG

R U S S I A N   Z O N E

A M E R I C A N   Z O N E

WIESBADEN

RHEIN MAIN

OPERATING ROUTES OF THE BERLIN AIRLIFT

to secure European security was through the rehabilitation of Germany.

A Revitalized Germany

In the years immediately after World War II, the United States administration came to the same conclusion and decided that Germany must be rebuilt in economic and political terms so that it could play its part in creating a strong Europe. The U.S. adopted the position that Germany should not be deindustrialized. Without an industrial base, the German economy would effectively be destroyed and would demand the injection of vast quantities of Western (and by implication, American) resources just to prevent the population from starving. This decision brought the allies into disagreement with the Soviets, who believed that Germany should be stripped of its production capabilities and also pay vast reparations to compensate the U.S.S.R. for its losses in World War II. was designed to replace the inflationary

The Douglas DC-3 was the most important airliner of the 1930s; some 430 civil aircraft were produced before the United States' entry into World War II. From this pioneering type the company evolved the parallel C-47 Skytrain and R4D transports for the U.S. Army Air Corps (soon the U.S. Army Air Force) and U.S. Naval Aviation respectively. More than 10,000 of these aircraft were built for military use, and many were transferred to the Royal Air Force. The British gave this great plane the name "Dakota" by which it is now almost universally known. The USAAF also used a number of impressed civil aircraft with designations ranging between C-48 and C-52, while a purely military model produced for the movement of personnel rather than the transport of troops and/or freight had the designation C-53 Skytrooper. The C-47 itself was produced in a number of variants with different engines and a number of other modifications making them suitable for specialist tasks such as paratroop dropping and assault glider towing, but externally they were all quite similar. Vast numbers of the C-47 were dumped onto an eager civil market after World War II, and it remained in widespread American service even though it was

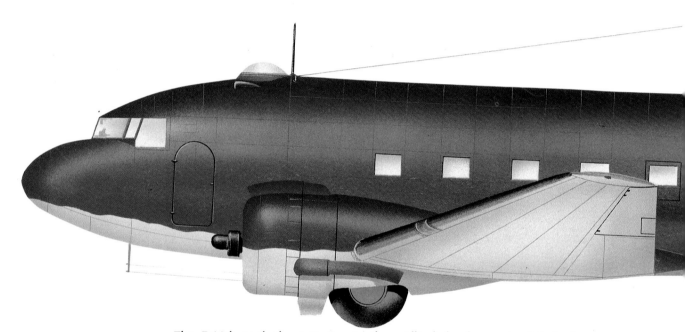

The British took the initiative in the rehabilitation of Germany, establishing in their zone a free press and trade unions, and laying the foundations for new political institutions. The Americans and French followed this lead. After the U.K. and the U.S. had merged their zones, the French joined this grouping, and the three Western Allies began to create a new federal state in western Germany. At the same time, the three occupying powers undertook currency reform, which set the financial system of western Germany on a path to stability and strength.

In the eastern zone, the U.S.S.R. followed a completely independent political path. It created inflationary havoc by printing vast sums of money unbacked by any hard resources or industrial growth. The U.S.S.R. understood that the Western

Allies' development of their three zones was leading toward the creation of a new nation, and West Germany was established as the Federal Republic of Germany on September 7, 1949, with Bonn its capital. France, the U.K., and the U.S. guaranteed the defense of West Germany on September 19, just four days after the election of Dr. Konrad Adenauer as West Germany's first chancellor. On September 21 military government ended.

The Soviets did what they could to disrupt these developments with a number of objections, but their main area of concern was the effect that the currency reforms would have on their own position in Berlin, nestled 100 miles inside the Soviet zone of Germany. The basic monetary reform was the introduction of the new Deutschmark, which supplemented by larger four-engined transports. Comparatively small numbers were converted for use as aerial gunships during the Vietnam War; these AC-47s soon acquired the nickname "Puff the Magic Dragon." The type disappeared from service only in the later 1970s. The C-47 was an all-metal airplane with a low-set wing whose two nacelles accommodated radial piston engines driving variable-pitch propellers. The nacelles also supported the main landing gear units, which retracted rearward but left the lower half of each wheel projecting to cushion the impact in a wheels-up landing. The C-47 was powered by two 1,200-horsepower (895-kW) Pratt & Whitney R-1830-92 radials, and on this power could carry a crew of two and a payload of 27 troops, or 10,000 pounds (4,536 kg) of freight, or between 18 and 24 stretchers for casualties. The maximum speed was 230 miles per hour (370 km/h), the service ceiling was 24,000 feet (7,315 m), and the range was 1,600 miles (2,575 km). Empty and maximum take-off weights were 18,200 and 26,000 pounds (8,256 and 11,794 kg) respectively, and the plane's dimensions included a span of 95 feet 6 inches (29·11 m) and a length of 63 feet 9 inches (19·43 m).

replaced the Reichsmark at the rate of one for ten. Linked with this economic factor was the feeling of the Soviet dictator Joseph Stalin, that the Western Allies' move toward a western German state was incompatible with the continued existence of a four-power arrangement in Berlin. Stalin therefore decided on a program of harassment designed to force the Western Allies into abandoning their zones in Berlin.

The Soviets Move to Isolate Berlin

On March 20, 1948, the Soviet delegation walked out of the Allied Control Council. On March 31, the Soviets announced that, from the following day, all surface traffic into Berlin would be subject to inspection by Soviet guards. The Western powers refused to concede the Soviet right to do this and cancelled all surface transportation except food and freight trains. On June 16, the Soviet representative walked out of the Komandatura (four-power military commission for the government of Berlin), effectively severing relations between the Soviets and the three Western powers in Berlin. At midnight on June 18, the Soviets banned all passenger traffic into Berlin by surface transport.

This harassment failed to produce the desired effect. On June 24, therefore, the Soviets stepped up their effort by cutting the rail links connecting the western zones of Berlin with western Germany. The pretext for this severance was "technical trouble," which was created when the Soviets themselves tore up 100 yards of track on each line to make sure that no trains could run the Soviet gauntlet.

Berlin was isolated from the west, and

its 2,500,000 inhabitants were left with enough food for less than a month. The Western Allies were apparently faced with two choices: stay in Berlin and starve together with the Berliners, or evacuate their forces and leave the western half of Berlin and the Berliners to the mercies of Soviet rule. Political and humanitarian considerations ruled out any abandonment of western Berlin, so the only other possibility was a massive airlift to fly in the food and other supplies needed by western Berlin.

An Airlift Feasible?

General Lucius D. Clay, the governor of the American zones in Germany, broached the subject to his air commander in an unusual way: "Can you transport coal by air?" After asking for the question to be repeated, Major General Curtis LeMay, commander of the U.S. Air Forces in Europe, replied with the assertion that "The Air Force can deliver anything." To meet the needs of western Berlin, the Western Allies had three air corridors into the city, each 20 miles wide, terminating at undeveloped Tegel in the northern French zone, Gatow in the central British zone, and Tempelhof in the American southern zone.

The planners calculated that an air bridge would have to supply western Berlin with 2,000 tons of food and other supplies each day. The delivery of this daily tonnage presented daunting difficulties. At the time that the Soviets launched what was in effect their siege of Berlin, LeMay had only 102 medium-sized Douglas C-47 Skytrain twin-engined transports, each able to carry a two-

Tempelhof

For further references
see pages
10, 15, 17, 18, *21*

During World War II, the Royal Air Force's equivalent to the Boeing B-17 Flying Fortress heavy bomber was the Avro Lancaster. But whereas the American bomber was designed for daylight operations at high altitude, using their superb Norden bombsights for attacks on pinpoint targets such as German ball-bearing factories and oil plants, the British bomber was intended for night operations at medium altitude, using optical and radar bombing techniques for the devastation of area targets such as German cities. The Lancaster remained in limited bomber service after World War II, but it's participation in the Berlin airlift was limited to a pair of derivatives, the York and Lancastrian. The York was a military transport based closely on the Lancaster but fitted with a large rectangular fuselage, while the Lancastrian was a Lancaster conversion with a revised fuselage interior and its nose, dorsal, and tail turrets removed and replaced with aerodynamic fairings.

ton load, and two larger Douglas C-54 Skymaster four-engined transports each able to lift a ten-ton load. This translated into 1,500 C-47 flights to arrive every day in Berlin. Only Gatow and Tempelhof airfields could cope with sustained air operations. The British could contribute a small number of transports, but it was clear that the air capability was far too low to deliver the necessary quantities.

The Airlift Starts

Scraping together every available airplane for what became Operation "Vittles," the Americans were able to begin the airlift on June 26 with the delivery of just 80 tons to Tempelhof. Two days later, the British Royal Air Force began its smaller, but nonetheless useful, contribution. Its deliveries to Gatow were initially serviced by 64 Douglas Dakotas (as the British called the C-47). The British crews were reinforced by Australian, New Zealand,

and South African personnel, and in the following weeks virtually the whole of RAF Transport Command's aircraft strength was allocated to the operation.

In the two weeks after June 28, the Americans and British established the basic form of the airlift, although deliveries were wholly inadequate for the longer-term survival of western Berlin. Yet the Soviets were clearly worried about the Western Allies' ability to sustain and expand the airlift; soon Soviet fighters were intruding into the air corridors flown by the transports and making aggressive passes at them.

The airlift was not the only way in which the United States responded to the intensification of the "Cold War" which began with the Soviet blockade of western Berlin. Overt military responses included a strengthening of the U.S. bomber capability in Europe. The single squadron of Boeing B-29 Superfortress bombers of the 301st Bombardment Group located at Furstenfeldbruck, near the German city of Munich in the American zone, was strengthened by the group's other two squadrons. Sixty aircraft from another two B-29 groups were moved from the United States to British bases. The U.S. Air Force announced that a wing of Lockheed F-80 Shooting Star fighters was

Curtis Le May

For further references
see pages
13, 14

Designed to replace
the C-47, the C-54 was
an altogether more
effective and
longer-range transport
with four engines and
tricycle landing gear.
The type was the
mainstay of the
American effort in the
Berlin airlift.

being relocated to western Germany from the Panama Canal Zone. On July 20, 16 F-80 fighters of the 56th Fighter Group arrived in England after staging from Selfridge Air Force Base, Michigan, on their way to Furstenfeldbruck.

Increased Daily Requirements

By this time, the U.S. Air Forces in Europe command was delivering more than 1,000 tons to Berlin on a daily basis, in what was jokingly called the "LeMay Coal & Feed Delivery Service." But it was becoming clear that the initial estimate of 2,000 tons of food and other supplies every day was too low. The Soviet siege was obviously going to be a protracted effort to force the Western Allies out of Berlin, which meant that emergency situations and the additional requirements of winter would have to be added into the equation. The U.S. planners soon con-

cluded that the daily total of 2,000 tons would have to be more than doubled, to 4,500 tons a day. The delivery of this tonnage was considered essential: only then would the Western Allies be able to stockpile enough food and fuel to guarantee western Berlin's survival through the winter, when adverse weather would inevitably affect the smooth pattern of daily deliveries.

This raised the question of who should run the operation. LeMay was essentially a combat commander, and his U.S. Air Forces in Europe was basically a combat command. It would be far better, many senior American commanders thought, to entrust the operation to the Military Air Transport Service, which was by its very nature a specialist in air transport matters. The allocation of the airlift to the Military Air Transport Service would allow the introduction of specialist planners and larger numbers of aircraft to the operation. It would also free LeMay and

William Tunner

For further references
see pages
14, 15, 16

A C-54 being loaded
with supplies bound
for Berlin. The flow of
aircraft continued
through all but the very
worse weather.

his men for combat operations should the Soviets use more than harassment to try to stem the flow of supplies into western Berlin.

A New Organization and a New Commander

The Military Air Transport Service was given responsibility for "Vittles," and on the instructions of U.S. Air Force Headquarters the Air Lift Task Force (Provisional) was set up on July 23. Command was entrusted to Major General William H. Tunner, whose new organization was allocated eight transport squadrons with a total of 72 C-54 aircraft. Arriving in western Germany, Tunner was greeted by LeMay with the words "I expect you to produce." The new commander's pithy answer was "I intend to."

Tunner's first task was an assessment of the current airlift effort, and he soon concluded that it was "a real cowboy operation." As a transport specialist, Tunner found that LeMay's airlift organization was hopelessly inefficient. Flight crews and ground crews alike were unscheduled; the C-47 transports were now in poor condition after sustained flights with no more than extemporized maintenance. Maintenance time was therefore high, aircraft utilization was low, and the air routes were restrictive.

Tempelhof and Gatow were only four minutes apart by air and within easy reach of no fewer than seven Soviet airfields. There was little or no room to maneuver, holding patterns operated above each airfield, and Templehof's capacity was inadequate because instead of properly paved runways, it had pierced steel planking laid by LeMay's men over the Germans' grass strips.

Tunner knew that the key to success was the maximum utilization of a smaller number of large aircraft in preference to a greater total of small aircraft. This simplified air-traffic control and ground handling, but increased the maintenance requirements, since each plane would run through its cycle of takeoffs and landings more rapidly. Another factor that Tunner took into consideration was the distance between the departure and arrival points used by the Western Allies. It was 290 miles from the American departure point at Rhein-Main, near Frankfurt-am-Main in the American zone, and Tempelhof in the American zone of Berlin; yet it was only 160 miles from the British departure points of Celle and Fassberg to Gatow in the British zone of Berlin. Logic showed that two aircraft based at Celle or Fassberg could carry the same payload as three aircraft based at Rhein-Main.

Tunner approached the British, and from August 21 U.S. aircraft were operating from Fassberg. Further integration followed on October 15, when the American and British airlifts were merged under the Combined Air Lift Task Force (Provisional) commanded by Tunner with a British officer, Air Commodore J.W.F. Mercer, as his second-in-command.

Tunner phased the C-47s out of the operation as soon as they could be replaced by larger aircraft. For the American part of "Vittles," this meant the C-54, of which some 275 were gleaned from various parts of the world for use in western Germany; the navy also contributed 24 of its R5D version. The only other American aircraft to participate in "Vittles" were one Douglas C-74 which made a single round trip, and five Fairchild C-82 Packets, whose layout allowed them to carry large vehicles loaded through the clam-shell rear doors of the fuselage "pod." The British used a number of larger transports, including the Avro York and Handley Page Hastings four-engined transports; and for a short time, some Short Sunderland flying boats flew into the Havelsee, a lake near the Berlin suburb of Spandau. The Sunderland had been designed for open-sea operations, and because it could survive salt corrosion, it was used to carry salt into Berlin.

American ground personnel refuel and check Douglas C-54 Skymaster transports before another flight into Berlin. The Skymaster was the mainstay of the American effort in this operation, which symbolized the determination of the American-led Western alliance to resist all efforts by the Soviets to extend their area of domination in Europe.

Gatow

For further references
see pages
10, 14, 16, 18

Steadily Increasing Daily Tonnage

The British effort involved 100 aircraft on average, including a number of civil aircraft under military contract. The American effort averaged 300 C-54s, of which 225 were in service and the other 75 under maintenance at any one time. The airlift to Berlin averaged more than 2,000 tons a day in July, rose to 3,839 tons a day during September, and reached more than 4,600 tons a day in October.

Under Turner's leadership, the Combined Air Lift Task Force (Provisional) maximized its use of the three available corridors. The southern corridor from the two main American bases of Wiesbaden and Rhein-Main was used only for flights into Templehof, while the central corridor from Gatow and Tempelhof to Wunstorf, Celle, Fassberg, and other airfields in the British zone of western Germany was reserved for outgoing flights. The only corridor that was used for two-way traffic was therefore the most northerly, which connected Gatow and Tegel with the airfields in the British zone of western Germany. Here, traffic was separated by height as well as distance to avoid the dangers of collision. The complexity of the corridor is indicated by the fact that the 1,000-foot altitude was reserved for aircraft flying from Tegel to Fuhlsbuttel and Schleswigland, the 1,500-foot altitude for aircraft flying from Fuhlsbuttel and Schleswigland to Tegel, and the 2,000-foot and the 2,500-foot altitude also for aircraft flying from Fassberg to Tegel. The 3,000-foot altitude was reserved for emergency flights, the 3,500-foot

A ground handling crew unload a 25-ton load of flour from a Douglas C-74 Globemaster heavy transport.

altitude for aircraft flying from Wunstorf to Gatow, the 4,000-foot altitude for aircraft flying from Celle to Gatow, the 4,500-foot altitude also for aircraft flying from Celle to Gatow, the 5,000-foot altitude for British commercial aircraft flying from Fuhlsbuttel to Gatow, and the 5,500-foot altitude for aircraft flying from Lubeck to Gatow.

For ease of communication, all flights to Berlin were coded "Easy" and all those from Berlin "Willie." All C-54 flights were "Big," so a C-54 bound for Berlin was "Big Easy." A comparable system of reporting names for loads was also adopted, with civilian loads known as "New York," military loads as "Chicago," and construction loads as "Engineer."

A Typical "Vittles" Flight

A typical flight from Wiesbaden provides good evidence of the precision to which

the operation was honed by Tunner and his team. The crew was given a specific departure time accurate to the second, the radio call signs and tail numbers of the three aircraft in front of it and the two behind it, and a weather briefing that was updated at 30-minute intervals. This last was made possible by a report from the radio operator of every seventh Berlin-bound plane. After boarding and completing the pre-flight checks, the crew started the engines, taxied out to the runway, and began the take-off right on schedule. The climb was undertaken at 500 feet per minute, and the crew then started on the precisely defined procedure intended to ease the plane into the right "slot" in the procession of aircraft using the corridor to Berlin. The plane flew over Darmstradt and Aschaffenberg, and then turned onto the bearing for the beacon at Fulda, the last in the American zone. As his airplane crossed over the Fulda beacon, the pilot broadcast the

Just seventeen minutes after arrival in Berlin, these four Douglas C-54 Skymaster transports were soon loaded for the return flight to an air base in the western part of Germany.

identification of his machine, allowing the pilots of the following aircraft to check their watches and make sure that they were the correct distance behind. From the Fulda beacon, the pilot headed straight for Tempelhof range station at exactly 170 miles per hour. At the range station, he wheeled left to the beacon at Wedding and started his landing procedures. At the Wedding beacon, the pilot turned his plane downwind and started reducing altitude to 1,500 feet as he turned onto final approach. After landing, the pilot followed the "Follow-Me" jeep and halted on the designated ramp section. The crew disembarked to be greeted by an operations officer with return-flight clearance and a weather briefing. German citizens and displaced persons unloaded the cargo straight into trucks as the crew received coffee, doughnuts, and snacks from a German Red Cross jeep.

Total turnaround time was only 30 minutes, one of Tunner's greatest achievements. He insisted that the crew be "watered and foddered" by their machine, rather than going to the terminal, and that unloading be done by those who would gain the greatest benefit from the operation's success.

Total Standardization

Tunner and his subordinates were firm believers in the standardization of everything that could be standardized. This simplified administration and streamlined operations, and it gave the least possible

Operation "Little Vittles" supplied the children of Berlin with over 150,000 candy bars. This young German girl has a bar of chocolate that had been dropped by a simple parachute.

chance for mistakes. The effort began with standardized training for pilots at the "Little Corridor" school at Great Falls, Montana. Each airplane had a completely standardized instrument panel and controls. The crew was standardized as a pilot, copilot, and flight engineer. The takeoff, climb, cruise, descent, and landing procedures were also standardized.

As far as possible, weather limits were standardized, too. Around Tempelhof there were tall apartment buildings, so the minima included a 400-foot cloud base and one-mile visibility, while for Gatow the minima were a 200-foot cloud base and half a mile visibility. Any pilot who missed his approach was directed straight into departure, generally to his home base, as there were no go-arounds and no stacking of planes, even in the worst weather.

The dispatch rate was one plane every three minutes, which meant that the runways at Tempelhof and Gatow were in use every 90 seconds for alternating touch-downs and takeoffs. In the corridors, the aircraft were confined to a precise speed and heading, and flew with a 500-foot vertical gap between the planes in every group of three: the first plane flew at 2,000 feet, the second at 2,500 feet three minutes behind the first, and the third at 3,000 feet three minutes behind the second. The leading plane of the next three-aircraft group back at 2,000 feet was another three minutes behind.

Heavy Maintenance Requirements

The C-54s flew an average of 8 hours 30 minutes every day. This high usage inevitably had an effect on the machines, and the problem was compounded by the

Inside the hold of a Boeing C-97 Stratofreighter.

Berliners celebrate the arrival of the first truckload of oranges after the Soviets had appreciated their failure and finally lifted the blockade of West Berlin.

high rate of takeoff and landing cycles. The Skymaster had been designed for long-range flights with comparatively few cycles per flight hour and a touch-down weight of some 63,500 pounds instead of the airlift's 71,000 pounds after takeoff at 72,000 pounds. Tires and engines wore out far more quickly than would otherwise have been the case, and finding replacement tires and engines became a major task for squadron supply officers, who had the difficult task of maintaining a C-54 force that needed some 90 engines and 700 tires every month.

Another difficulty was lack of adequate maintenance personnel, but this problem was circumvented (despite the Western Allies' policy of "non-fraternization" with the Germans) by the use of ex-Luftwaffe personnel supervised by General Hans Detlev von Rodhen. This officer translated the relevant manuals, and by the end of the airlift, there were more German than American personnel working on the C-54 fleet.

When a C-54 had completed 200 hours of airlift work, it was flown to a base at Burtonwood in England for an inspection. After four inspections, the plane was loaded with engines needing repair, and flown by a Military Air Transport Service ferry crew across the North Atlantic to Westover Air Force Base, Massachusetts. The cargo of engines was unloaded and shipped to the relevant repair facility, and the plane then flew to one of four civilian centers for a 44-day overhaul. Then the plane was returned to service, flying across the North Atlantic once more with a payload of spares and repaired engines.

A French Contribution

The tonnage of freight that was delivered into Berlin continued to rise, especially after the French made the airfield of Tegel in their zone available. A Soviet radio tower was an approach hazard to this field, but the Soviets refused to consider its removal. To celebrate the opening of the airfield, the French threw a party for the Americans and British, and in mysterious circumstances, the tower was explosively demolished during the party!

It finally became clear to the Soviets that they were not going to starve the

three western zones of Berlin into submission. In fact, the airlift was so successful that, during the winter, it became possible to increase the rations of the Berliners. On May 9, 1948, the Soviet military governor announced that the blockade would end at two minutes after midnight on May 12. The Americans and British did not tempt fate by ending the airlift immediately, but kept it going to supplement deliveries via the reopened land routes and to build up a reserve in case the Soviets imposed an embargo once more.

During the summer, the airlift was gradually scaled down, and it ended on September 30. It had been an incredible effort that had resulted in the delivery of almost one ton for every Berliner. Except for one period of 15 hours in November 1948, when heavy fog prevented all air operations, "Vittles" had continued for 24 hours every day, for seven days every week. The best day was April 16, 1949, when an "Easter Parade" schedule saw the delivery of 12,940 tons in 1,398 flights. In overall terms, the operation's 277,264 flights delivered 2,325,809 tons of supplies, including 1,586,530 tons of coal, 92,282 tons of liquid fuel, and 538,016 tons of food. Of the total, U.S. military aircraft moved some 1,783,000 tons and British

military and civil aircraft the other 542,800 or so tons.

Huge Success for "Vittles"

Despite its intensity, the weather, serviceability problems, and constant harassment by the Soviets, "Vittles" had proved a remarkable testament to the capabilities and safety of air transport. Under these far from perfect operating conditions, the operation cost the lives of relatively few men; the total of 75 deaths among American and British airmen included the crash of a British transport that was hit by a Soviet plane which was harassing it.

The airlift had the important effect of maintaining the western zones of Berlin against Soviet pressure and served notice on the U.S.S.R. that the United States and United Kingdom would not be pushed around. The airlift had an important secondary effect, moreover: it materially affected the perception of the Americans and British about the Germans. From this point on, western Germany was increasingly seen as a bastion of the West against Soviet aggression, and this changed attitude was one of the reasons for the Allied

A line of Douglas C-47s disgorges supplies for the beleaguered citizens of West Berlin. During the main part of the airlift, American and British aircraft were landing at one of the city's airfields at the rate of one plane every 61·8 seconds.

Airmen of navy squad VR-6 greet an aircrew after they had delivered 10 tons of supplies to Tempelhof at the end the blockade.

agreement establishing the Federal Republic of Germany on September 7, 1949.

However, although the Soviets ended their siege of Berlin, they did not terminate their policy of harassing American, British and, to a lesser extent, French aircraft over Berlin and the border between the eastern and western zones of Germany. Incident followed incident as the Soviets and their East German puppets tested the resolve of the Western allies.

The Lebanese Intervention (1958)

Up to 1864, Lebanon was part of the province of Syria within the Ottoman Empire, a once powerful, but now a crumbling edifice ruled with a loose hand from Istanbul. In that year, Lebanon (or more formally Mount Lebanon) was separated from Syria into a self-governing region. With the dissolution of the Ottoman Empire after World War I, Lebanon was placed under French mandate. In 1940, Lebanon was held by the forces of Vichy France (the rump of France left by the German occupation of northern and eastern France during the early stages of World War II), but was captured by the British in 1941. For the rest of World War II, Lebanon was occupied by British and Free French forces, but it became independent in 1946 when the British and French troops were withdrawn.

Although Lebanon had been a self-governing region of the Ottoman Empire, the French had created the modern Lebanon after World War I by combining the predominantly Christian area of Turkish Lebanon (mainly the region between Beirut in the south and Tripoli in the north) with the predominantly Islamic areas farther north and south along the eastern coast of the Mediterranean, and the inland area to the east of the Christian area. This amalgamation set up a somewhat artificial country with equal numbers of Christians and Moslems, but the Christians held economic and political power. While the Moslems were supported by Syria this fact inevitably produced friction between the two groups. Between 1946 and 1958, a

Photographed in the early months of 1946 in the immediate aftermath of World War I, Beirut was a beautiful city with a prosperous harbor. This was soon to change radically for the worse as Lebanon gained independence from France, the European power that had controlled the country under a League of Nations' mandate received after World War I.

precarious peace was maintained, with the most untoward incident being a rebellion that arose but was quickly suppressed in July 1949.

By the late 1950s, both Christians and Moslems were becoming weary of the Maronite Christian administration of President Camille Chamoun, who had fallen foul of both groups because of his support of France and the U.K. during the Suez campaign of 1956, and for political maneuvrings designed to extend his presidency beyond its legal term. These rumblings of discontent might not have reached crisis point if a revolutionary pan-Arab movement, which helped to stir up anger in the Moslem population, had not taken a clandestine hand. One catalyst that helped turn discontent into a desire for an Arab nation was the creation of the United Arab Republic on February 1, 1958. This agreement linked the Egypt of Colonel Gamal Abdel Nasser with Syria

and Yemen, which Nasser saw as the beginning of an Arab state that would dominate the Middle East.

On April 14, 1958, the Moslems of Tripoli rose against Chamoun's government, and by the middle of the following month, the rebellion had spread to the Moslems of Beirut and Sidon and to the Shi'a Moslems of the Baalbek region of the upper Bekaa valley. Syrian forces occupied several border regions in support of the Moslem rebels and an observer team from the United Nations arrived under the Secretary General, Dag Hammerskjold, but it seemed to Chamoun that Lebanon was being abandoned to its fate.

On July 14, again with the hand of Nasser evident, the Iraqi army rose under Brigadier General Abdul Karim el Kassim to overthrow the government of King Faisal II, who was brutally murdered together with his prime minister, Nuri es Said. Fearing that his small country was

Since the end of World War II, men of the U.S. Army's airborne formations have been among the first to contribute to any American force. Here Brigadier General David W. Gray, commander of the 24th Airborne Brigade, prepares to leave from a Lockheed C-130 Hercules transport in the first major drop of American paratroopers into Beirut in July 1958. This drop totaled 360 men of the 24th Airborne Brigade, supported by elements of the 1st Airborne Battle Group, 187th Parachute Infantry Regiment.

Men of the 1st Airborne Battle Group, 187th Parachute Infantry Regiment, exit from their Lockheed C-130 Hercules transport to descend on "Sahara" Drop Zone on the edge of Beirut airport. Once they had landed, the paratroopers moved into defensive tactical positions, allowing American transports to fly into the airport with reinforcements.

now about to fall completely under the sway of an ever more powerful United Arab Republic, Chamoun asked France, the United Kingdom, and the United States for military support. At the same time, King Hussein of Jordan called for similar aid to secure his country from the internal threat of communism coupled with the external threat posed by Iraq and Syria. The British responded to the Jordanian call, landing airborne forces that received considerable American air and logistical support.

Chamoun's request for assistance was couched in terms of sealing the Lebanese frontier with Syria to isolate the country from the flames of pan-Arab nationalism that seemed to be sweeping the majority of the Middle East. President Dwight D. Eisenhower decided that the American forces should respond, though not to the extent demanded by Chamoun.

President Camille Chamoun

For further references see pages
23, 28, 29

Beirut

For further references see pages
22, *23*, 25, *26*, *27*, 28, *29*, *30*, *31*, *32*, *101*, 103, *105*, *107*, *109*, 110

Enter the Marines

The most readily available combat troops were three U.S. Marine Corps battalion landing teams and a provisional brigade headquarters, providentially embarked on ships of the Mediterranean-based 6th Fleet for a landing exercise. On July 15, Battalion Landing Team 2/2 (the 2nd Battalion of the 2nd Marine Regiment) landed south of Beirut and soon secured a beachhead that included Beirut Airport. On the following day, Battalion Landing Team 3/6 came ashore and moved into Beirut to secure land communications

With the area around Beirut airport safely in American hands so that reinforcements could be flown in, heavier equipment and weapons could be landed from American ships lying off the Lebanese shore. Photographed on August 4, 1958, this M48 battle tank is being lifted out of the hold of the new vehicle cargo ship *Comet* before being lowered into an LSM (Landing Ship, Medium) for delivery onto the beach adjacent to Beirut airport.

Opposite Top Left: An M48 battle tank of the 35th Armored Battalion arrives on the Lebanese beach from a landing craft on August 4, 1958. There was no real operational role for these vehicles in the absence of an enemy with fighting vehicles, but their presence in Lebanon gave the U.S. Army the potential for heavy operations should the need arise.

Left: With U.S. forces increasing their control over Beirut and its neighboring areas, the full weight of the American logistics machine swung into action to guarantee that the men on the ground had all the equipment they needed. This photograph, taken on August 15, 1958, shows a gas tanker of the army's 109th Transportation Regiment being unloaded from the merchant ship S.S. *Harry Culbreath* of the Lykes Lines.

Below: Further support for the American forces in Lebanon arrived by air, in this instance via a Douglas C-124 Globemaster II. The two-deck Globemaster II provided easy access to the lower deck via clamshell doors in its lower nose, and in addition to its eight-man crew could carry 68,500 pounds (31,072 kg) of freight including light vehicles, or alternatively 200 passengers or 127 stretchers.

Above Right: Men and trucks of the 299th Combat Engineer Regiment arrive in Beirut on August 7, 1958.

Right: A U.S. Army truck is swayed ashore from the S.S. *African Patriot*, the first merchantman to arrive in Beirut harbor with American supplies on July 25, 1958.

Below: Men of the U.S. Army bring jeeps and other headquarters equipment up from the beach where they had been landed from a navy LCU (Landing Craft, Utility).

27

between the beachhead and the U.S. embassy. One day later still, Battalion Landing Team 1/8 landed north of Beirut. During the same day, the leading elements of the 2nd Battalion, 8th Marine Regiment, arrived by air from Camp Lejoune, North Carolina, as the first component of an American commitment that soon included airborne, tank, and combat engineer forces provided by the U.S. Army from its strength in Europe. The first army unit to arrive was an airborne brigade, whose commanding officer assumed overall command of the U.S. forces in Lebanon.

From the beginning of the operation, however, it was made clear that the American commitment was not designed to bolster Chamoun's regime, but to prevent the fall of Lebanon to communist aggression.

By the end of July, these forces had been bolstered by additional units from within the United States and had stabilized the situation along the Lebanese coast. Additional strength was provided by the 6th Fleet warships patrolling off the Lebanese coast and by the Composite Air Strike Force that arrived at various Turkish air bases to provide powerful air support if the ground forces needed more aerial firepower than the 6th Fleet's aircraft carrier could give. These moves effectively curtailed the rebellion even before the U.S. ground commitment reached its peak strength

General Randolph M. Pate, Commandant of the U.S. Marine Corps, talks to the marine crew of an M50 Ontos vehicle in Lebanon. By the standards of the day, these weapons were indifferent in their intended antitank role, but could deliver devastating and demoralizing support fire for infantry stalled in front of obstacles such as machine gun nests and other strongpoints.

of 5,800 marines and 8,500 soldiers.

This prompt reaction by the American and British governments allowed the Lebanese and Jordanian governments to restore order in their respective countries. By the middle of August, it was clear that the Lebanese crisis was over, and from August 21, the 14,300 Americans left in a withdrawal that was completed on October 25. Sporadic fighting had continued over the first part of the American involvement, but the replacement of Chamoun by General Chehab during September marked the effective end of the Moslem uprising.

Wide-ranging Ramifications

In the aftermath of this crisis, both the Lebanese and Jordanian governments became recipients of special American military assistance to build up their forces with equipment and training that would, it was hoped, prevent any recurrence of these events. In any case, Lebanon and Jordan were able to feel more secure after the dissolution of the United Arab Republic: Syria split away from the republic on September 30, 1961; Iraq never integrated itself with the republic and soon diverged; and on

An M48 battle tank of the 35th Armored Regiment and an infantryman of Company ''C,'' 187th Infantry Regiment, are seen on roadblock duty near Beirut on August 22, 1958.

Left: Men of the Headquarters Platoon, Heavy Mortar Battery, 187th Airborne Brigade, man a machine gun position protecting the entrance to a tunnel running under the main runway of Beirut airport.

Below: M48 battle tanks of the 3rd Medium Tank Battalion, 35th Armored Regiment, marshall on the edge of Beirut airport.

Above Left: Men of the U.S. Army man a recoilless rifle position dominating the railroad line that skirted the edge of the American bivouac position in Beirut.

Above Right: A Sikorsky H-34 Choctaw transport helicopter of the Aviation Battalion, 24th Airborne Brigade, unloads men of Company ''C,'' 1st Airborne Battle Group, 187th Parachute Infantry Regiment near Byblos on the Lebanese coast during a training exercise in which 200 men were delivered by helicopter.

Right: The platoon sergeant of the 1st Platoon, 3rd Medium Tank Battalion, 35th Armored Regiment, briefs his men before a M48 battle tank patrol around the perimeter of Beirut airport.

December 26, 1961, Egypt broke with the Yemeni monarchy and gave its support to the country's republican rebels.

The whole episode had other repercussions for the United States after Iraq withdrew from the Baghdad Treaty on March 24, 1959. More formally known as the Middle East Treaty Organization, signed in 1955, this agreement was a mutual-defense arrangement between Iran, Iraq, Pakistan, Turkey, and the United Kingdom. The United States initially declined to participate, but established observer status at the organization's first meeting on November 21, 1955. It became a partial participant on April 19, 1956, and on March 5, 1959, signed treaties with the "Northern Tier" of Middle East Treaty Organization members, namely Iran, Pakistan, and Turkey.

The withdrawal of Iraq called for a new arrangement, and on October 27, 1959, the alliance was recast as the Central Treaty Organization, whose members were Iran, Pakistan, Turkey, and the United Kingdom, with the United States as a member of its economic, military, and anti-subversion committees.

Right: An M48 battle tank of the 3rd Medium Tank Battalion, 35th Armored Regiment, plows the remains of a rebel roadblock off a street in Beirut on October 9, 1958.

Below: U.S. military personnel move through Beirut by truck on their way from the harbor to the main bivouac area.

The Bay of Pigs Fiasco
(1961)

It has always been to American advantage to keep major military events as distant as possible from the continental United States, preferably far enough away that the Atlantic or Pacific oceans could serve as huge buffers. By a twist of fate, however, one of the greatest threats to face the United States during the period of the "Cold War" occurred right in the American backyard, namely the island nation of Cuba lying across the entrance to the Gulf of Mexico off the southern tip of Florida.

In March 1952, a military revolution had overthrown the government and allowed General Fulgencio Batista to establish a military dictatorship. The Batista regime was notoriously corrupt and inevitably produced a considerable resistance movement. Initially this resistance was poorly organized, but after Fidel Castro, a young communist, emerged as its leader, the movement began to gain cohesion. Castro was captured and imprisoned in 1953, released in a general amnesty in May 1955, and departed to Mexico to organize the overthrow of Batista. In November 1956, Castro landed with 81 men at Las Coloradas in Oriente province and moved into the rugged mountains of the nearby Sierra Maestra. By the summer of 1958, Castro had increased his rebel "army" considerably and dominated the Sierra Maestra region. In October 1958, Castro took the offensive, moving out through Cuba to the northwest. The revolutionary army swept all before it, and by the end of 1958, Batista had fled to the Dominican Republic, allowing Castro to enter Havana on January 1, 1959, as the liberator of Cuba. Castro soon created the beginnings of an orthodox communist state in the island, though many Cubans managed to escape, most of them to Florida.

These early exiles from the Cuban communist regime made several efforts to persuade President Eisenhower that the United States should invade Cuba and

Right: Fidel Castro came to power in Cuba after a successful revolution in 1959, and his communist regime in the United States' southern "backyard" has been a constant concern to the American government.

Fidel Castro

For further references see pages
33, 34, 38, 90

forcibly remove the Castro regime. Eisenhower was noncommittal rather than totally opposed, and in 1960 five of the splintered exile groups formed the Frente Revolucionario Democratico (revolutionary democratic front).

Worsening American-Cuban Relations

In June 1960, Castro nationalized the American and British oil refineries on Cuba because they had refused to process Soviet oil. In retaliation, the United States refused to take more than three-quarters of its annual sugar quota, and Castro responded in August by nationalizing all the island's private American companies at the same time that private Cuban companies were expropriated. The Central Intelligence Agency began to plan an intervention using Cuban exiles, and, in exchange for sugar, the Cuban government began to receive weapons from the U.S.S.R. and its eastern European satellites during late 1960. These weapons were perfectly

33

Fidel Castro shakes hands with Vice President Richard M. Nixon before the American government broke off relations with the new communist government of the island country.

conventional items such as tanks, antitank rocket launchers, field artillery, and antiaircraft weapons that considerably upgraded the Cuban army. At the same time, Castro revised the structure of the Cuban armed forces, which included the Fuerza Aerea Revolucionaro (revolutionary air force). This service operated a miscellany of obsolescent American and British aircraft while it awaited the arrival of more modern Soviet aircraft including Mikoyan-Gurevich MiG-15 and MiG-17 fighters. The Fuerza Aerea Revolucionaro operated from bases at San Antonio de los Lanos, Campo Lbertad, and Campo Columbia near Havana, and Camaguey, Holquin, San Julian, and Santiago de Chile elsewhere on the island.

Cuba had accused the United States of interference in Cuban affairs since 1959, and there was a considerable volume of inconclusive evidence to support this claim. For example, on November 29, 1959, aircraft had dropped anticommunist leaflets over Havana, and on March 4, 1960, the French ship *Le Coubre* blew up in Havana harbor while it was delivering munitions. Anticommunist guerrilla forces operating in Cuba were supported by air drops in Curtiss C-46 Commando twin-engined transports in fake markings flown by Central Intelligence Agency pilots.

The CIA: Adequate Player in a Complex Game?

The Central Intelligence Agency's operation against the Cuban government was masterminded by a specialized staff headed by Richard Bisell, the agency's deputy director of plans. This staff had considerable experience of such operations, including the 1954 overthrow of the Guatemalan government when the victorious rebels were supported by Republic P-47 Thunderbolt fighters in fake Guatemalan markings but flown by agency-paid mercenaries.

With the active support of the agency, the Frente Revolucionario Democratico had created an invasion force of some 1,000 Cuban exiles, and by late 1960 this unit was under intensive training at a secret base near Retalhuleu in Guatemala.

The Central Intelligence Agency worked

on the basis that an invasion had to be "plausibly deniable" by an American government effort and therefore worked through a number of fronts. The pilots, for example, were hired through the Double-Chek Corporation; most of them were pilots of the Alabama Air National Guard who normally worked for the Hayes International Corporation of Birmingham, Alabama. The chief of operations for the invasion was General Reid Doster, commander of the 117th Reconnaissance Wing of the Alabama Air National Guard. Other agency front companies included Intermountain Aviation, which operated on behalf of the Caribbean Marine Aero Corporation to buy Douglas B-26 Invader attack bombers from ex-air force stocks held at Tucson, Arizona; Southern Air Transport, which operated C-46 and Douglas C-54 Skymaster transports from Clewiston and Opa Locka Naval Air Station in Florida; and Interarmco, which supplied ex-government weapons, jeeps, trucks, and landing craft.

Plans Based on Belief in Cuban Opposition to Castro

The plan to invade Cuba and exploit the anticipated popular uprising against the communists was complete by March 1961, when the invasion force numbered about 1,400 men. By this time, John F. Kennedy had been inaugurated as the new president. Kennedy gave his approval to the scheme, which was based on the destruction of most of the Fuerza Aerea Revolucionaro's attack aircraft, followed by the invasion and supposed rising. To destroy the Cuban air force's main operational assets and provide a pretext for the landing, the Central Intelligence Agency planned that some of its B-26s would be painted in Cuban markings, fly from Nicaragua to bomb the Cuban air force's main bases, and then fly to Florida as though they were Cuban aircraft that were defecting after rallying the call for rebellion.

Early in the morning of April 15, 1961, eight B-26B attack bombers departed from Puerto Cabezas in Nicaragua, each carrying ten 260-pound bombs and eight 5-inch rockets in addition to its fixed machine gun armament. The aircraft divided into three flights to attack the airfields of San Antonio de los Lanos, Campo Libertad, and Havana's airport, Antonio Maceo. Warned of what was about to happen by their agents in the exile movement, the Cubans met the attackers with heavy antiaircraft fire. Even so, at San Antonio the attackers destroyed one Lockheed T-33 jet trainer and several B-26's before departing; one plane ran low on fuel and landed at Grand Cayman. At Campo Libertad, several ground installations were destroyed or damaged, and at Antonio Maceo, the attackers destroyed a Hawker Sea Fury fighter and a civilian Douglas DC-3; one of the attackers crashed into the sea and another landed at Boca Chica Naval Air Station on Key West with engine trouble.

Easily Perceived Deception

At mid-morning, a single B-26 landed at Miami International Airport and its pilot claimed that he was a Cuban pilot who had defected with several others after they had attacked their own airfields. However, a sharp-eyed reporter noticed that the airplane was a B-26, while the Cuban air force operated only the B-26C.

By this time, the invasion itself was under way as the invasion force, known as Brigade 2506, left Puerto Cabezas in five 2,400-ton Garcia Line vessels (the *Atlantico, Caribe, Houston, Lake Charles,* and *Rio Escondido*) supported by two infantry landing craft (the Barbara J and Blagar). Air support for the men of Brigade 2506 was to be provided by 24 B-26 attack bombers, and transport capability was entrusted to six C-46s and six C-54s.

On April 16, the B-26s were launched in an attack to soften up the landing area in the Bahia de Cochinos, or Bay of Pigs, on the southern coast of Cuba in Las Villas Province, southeast of Havana. Some targets were tackled, but the attackers lost two aircraft shot down (probably by T-33s), two crashed at sea, and one crash landed in Nicaragua on its return from the mission.

The invasion force entered the Bay of Pigs on April 17. As the Cuban exile

John F. Kennedy

For further references see pages 37, 38, 39, 41, 42, 47, 48, 63, 64 force landed, the *Houston* was bombed and sunk. The main insurrectionist force landed successfully, however, and soon consolidated a beachhead containing an airstrip long enough for C-46 operations. At this time, the men of Brigade 2506 were totally without air support, however, and were soon under attack from the surviving aircraft of the Cuban air force, which sank the *Rio Escondido* and hit the force on the beachhead. The surviving B-26 attack bombers from Nicaragua later attacked the positions of the Cuban forces massing against the exiles in the beachhead, but although they suffered no further losses, these aircraft were unable to check the buildup of the Cuban forces.

The Writing Is on the Wall

Further attacks were made on April 18, but already it was clear that there would be no popular uprising against the communists and that the invasion was therefore doomed. A last air attack was delivered in the morning of April 19. With considerable reluctance, Kennedy had authorized the use of navy aircraft to escort the B-26 attack bombers, but the bombers missed the escort of unmarked Douglas A4D-2 Skyhawks from the VA-86 squadron from the U.S.S. *Essex*. When the B-26s attacked, one was shot down by a T-33 and another by antiaircraft fire: of the 24 aircraft available on April 15, 12 had been lost (together with 14 crewmen killed or missing) in just five days of operations. The invasion force in the Bay of Pigs was mopped up by April 20. It lost 120 men killed and 1,200 captured; the remainder escaped, and some eventually managed to return to the United States.

The propaganda machine tried to pass off the episode as an attempt to resupply anticommunist guerrillas in the Escambray Mountains, but the whole episode was a disaster that humiliated the United States and seriously reduced the country's international standing at a time when it was already under intense Soviet pressure following the episode of Francis Gary Powers, who had been captured after his Lockheed U-2

Cuban communist troops and militiamen pose jubilantly with a launch captured from the American-backed force of Cuban insurgents during the "Bay of Pigs" fiasco.

"spyplane" was shot down near the Soviet city of Sverdlovsk during an illegal overflight of the U.S.S.R. in May 1960.

The American Position is Weakened

This weakening of the United States' international position could not have taken place at a worse time. Nikita Khrushchev, the Soviet premier who had ousted Nikolai Bulganin in March 1958, was due to meet President Kennedy in the Austrian capital of Vienna during June for tricky negotiations about Berlin, where the growing prosperity of the three western zones was in marked contrast to the drab poverty of the Soviet zone. Thus western Berlin was as much a thorn in the Soviet side as Cuba was an irritant to the United States. During 1958, Khrushchev had demanded that Berlin be made a free city. He issued a threat that unless Western troops were withdrawn within six months, the U.S.S.R. would reach a new accommodation with the German Democratic Republic, which had been created as a Soviet satellite on October 7, 1949, and was generally known in the West as East Germany. Khrushchev later backed away from his threat, and the United States concluded "wrongly" that this was evidence of a softening of the Soviet position. The Vienna summit of June 3-4, 1961, only six weeks after the Bay of Pigs catastrophe, showed that Khrushchev was just as intransigent as ever. Khrushchev warned Kennedy that unless the United States acceded to Soviet demands about Berlin, the U.S.S.R. would take unilateral action to solve this so-called problem. Kennedy refused to modify his position. He called the Soviet bluff, but came away from the meeting with the impression that continued peace was at best problematical.

Just over a month later, on July 10, the United States rejected a Soviet proposal that the Americans, British, and French should pull their forces out of western Berlin, which would then be garrisoned by a smaller force under the United Nations Organization.

Kennedy requested and received from Congress permission and funding to call 250,000 members of the Ready Reserve into federal service. The president considered but declined declaring a national emergency, which would have permitted him to bring one million reservists back into full federal service. Kennedy understood that although this might strengthen the U.S. forces at a time of great crisis, it might also worry the American public and, more threateningly, panic the Soviets into hasty over-reaction.

The "Berlin Wall"

The crisis deepened during the early part of August as thousands of East Germans crossed over into the western zones of Berlin. Embarrassed by the exodus and increasingly concerned about the economic impact that the loss of so many people might have on the East German economy, the communists closed the crossings from the Soviet zone on August 12. Virtually overnight, they built the infamous "Berlin Wall," to provide a secure physical barrier between the Soviet zone and the three Western ones. The Western powers protested at the border closure, but the U.S.S.R. rejected the protests on September 11.

Nikita Khrushchev

For further references see pages 39, 47, 48

East German workmen clear debris around a section of the "Berlin Wall," newly strengthened in December 1961 after it was erected earlier the same year.

American tanks and armored personnel carriers are pictured on the streets of West Berlin at the height of the Berlin Wall crisis.

During that month, President Kennedy made two decisions: that the number of American troops in Europe must be increased, and that the strength of the forces in the continental United States must be boosted by calling more reservists and even reserve units into federal service. By October, the strength of the regular army had been increased by 80,000 men, and more than 120,000 reservists (including two National Guard divisions) had been called into federal service.

Convinced that the United States meant business, the U.S.S.R. pressed matters no further, and from late 1961, the tension in Europe began to ease. By the middle of 1962, the reserve units had been stood down although the larger regular forces were maintained at this level.

With their European pressure more than answered by American determination and strength, the Soviets looked for another avenue along which pressure could be directed at the United States. They fixed their sights on Cuba, potentially the "Achilles heel" of the United States.

The Cuban Missile Crisis
(1962)

On May 1, 1961, Castro declared that Cuba was a socialist nation. On the following day, Secretary of State Dean Rusk responded with the assertion that Cuba had become a fully fledged member of the communist bloc. Castro had already called on the U.S.S.R. for more weapons, claiming that the United States still had designs on Cuba. By August 1962, American intelligence agencies had hard evidence of considerable Soviet arms shipments to Cuba; and on August 22, the director of the Central Intelligence Agency, John McCone, advised President Kennedy that a number of aircraft and large missiles had been included in recent Soviet shipments. The fear was that the aircraft could include nuclear-capable bombers, and the missiles might be medium-range ballistic weapons capable of carrying nuclear warheads.

The Central Intelligence Agency was

already flying U-2 sorties over Cuba to provide reconnaissance data on arms shipments, and these flights were stepped up in an effort to find hard evidence of Soviet intentions. At the same time, air force reconnaissance aircraft and navy patrol aircraft were ordered to pay special attention to Soviet shipping that might be ferrying weapons into Cuba.

On August 29, 1962, a U-2 reconnaissance flight secured photographic evidence of two SA-2 "Guideline" surface-to-air missile sites in Cuba, with another six in various stages of construction. The realization that these eight sites bore a remarkable similarity to the standard site used for protecting Soviet strategic missile complexes added urgency to the work of the photographic interpreters.

On September 4, President Kennedy announced that the military strength of Cuba's forces had been considerably boosted by the delivery of Soviet weapons and equipment, but that there was no concrete evidence of any significant offensive capability on the island. Over the next few days, the president came under increasing pressure for action from several members of Congress, most notably Senator Kenneth Keating, but on September 12, Kennedy said that he opposed any invasion of Cuba. On the following day, however, the president warned the U.S.S.R. that the United States would not tolerate the installation of Soviet offensive weapons on Cuba. Khrushchev replied with the assertion that the U.S.S.R. had no need to locate weapons in Cuba.

Soviet Missiles Begin to Arrive

Just four days later, a Lockheed P-2 Neptune long-range patrol airplane of the navy's VP-44 squadron photographed the Soviet freighter *Omsk* apparently headed for Havana: on the freighter's deck were large oblong containers, each the right size to contain a medium-range ballistic missile. The reconnaissance effort over Cuba was again increased. Oddly enough, on September 19, the U.S. Intelligence Board revealed its conclusion that the Soviets would not deploy nuclear missiles to Cuba, even though another shipment of possible missile containers had reached Havana only four days earlier.

The continuing reconnaissance overflights revealed additional construction work at potential missile sites, and on October 10 the air force's 4080th Strategic Reconnaissance Wing assumed responsibility for the reconnaissance effort, replacing the Central Intelligence Agency. The wing used the same U-2E aircraft with improved electronic countermeasures, and operated out of McCoy, Barksdale, and McLaughlin Air Force Bases. The ostensible reason for the air

Above: Operated by the Strategic Air Command and the Central Intelligence Agency, the Lockheed U-2 was the most important high-altitude strategic reconnaissance airplane operated by the United States in the late 1950s and early 1960s. Many were lost on clandestine flights; the most important loss from the political and military points of view was that piloted by Francis Gary Powers, shot down by a new surface-to-air missile near Sverdlovsk in the U.S.S.R.

Left: In the late 1950s and early 1960s, a time when the American forces were not involved in major overseas operations, considerable emphasis was placed on combined arms training. Seen here on their way to a joint army and air force exercise are a trio of RF-101 Voodoo photo-reconnaissance aircraft. This was a specialized derivative of the McDonnell F-101 interceptor and strike fighter with the nose modified to accommodate cameras behind optically flat windows.

force taking over the reconnaissance duties was the increased military threat posed by the SA-2 surface-to-air missiles; in fact, there was considerable dissatisfaction with the Central Intelligence Agency at this time because of its total failure in the Bay of Pigs episode and its partial failure during the Berlin crisis. The first air force flight, flown on the day that the service assumed responsibility, discovered the construction of roads associated with missile sites.

Opposite: A close-up of the underside of the McDonnell RF-101 Voodoo's nose reveals the camera windows of this photo-reconnaissance plane. Spare drop fuel tanks carried under the wing roots give it additional tactical range, much needed in the Cuban missile crisis, in which the Lockheed U-2 and RF-101 played key roles.

Below: A typical result of the reconnaissance missions over Cuba, this photograph shows MiG-21 fighters on Cienfuegos Airfield.

A Strategic Threat

Hurricane Ella caused a three-day gap before a U-2E lifted off again from Patrick Air Force Base on October 14. The plane flew over Cuba for just six minutes and took 928 photographs of two sites at San Cristobal and Sagua la Granda. Processing of the photographs was completed the following day, and the initial interpretation was so alarming that the prints were rushed straight to President Kennedy on October 16. What the prints showed was two medium-range ballistic missile sites at an advanced stage of construction, with some SS-4 "Sandal" missiles already deployed.

Irrefutable proof of Soviet intentions was now in American hands, and the Cuban Missile Crisis began, as the president set about guaranteeing the removal of the missiles from Cuba. As first steps, the president created an Executive Committee of the most powerful figures in the American government and ordered low-level reconnaissance flights so that better photographic evidence could be gathered. This latter task was entrusted to the McDonnell RF-101C Voodoo aircraft of the 29th Tactical Reconnaissance Squadron, based at Shaw Air Force Base, Alabama. They undertook their first sorties on October 17 and brought back even more disquieting information when they photographed sites at Guajanay and Remedios that gave the appearance of being designed for intermediate-range ballistic missiles. Whereas its 1,200-mile range gave a medium-range ballistic missile the ability to reach from Cuba to any point in the southeastern corner of the United States, its 2,000-mile range allowed a Cuban-based intermediate-range ballistic missile to touch any spot in virtually the whole eastern half of the country.

On October 18, President Kennedy attended a prearranged meeting with the Soviet foreign minister, Andrei Gromyko, and warned him that the moves seemed a direct threat to American security. Gromyko replied that the only Soviet weapons in Cuba were defensive systems. As the two leaders met, the Executive Committee was also in session to analyze Soviet intentions and discuss possible U.S. responses.

10 NOVEMBER 1962
MISSILE EQUIPPED AIRCRAFT
CAMILO CIENFUEGOS AIRFIELD, SANTA CLARA

FISHBEDS WITH MISSILES UNDER WINGS

Devious Soviet Intentions

The committee's conclusion was that the most likely Soviet intention was to put pressure on the United States for two purposes: probably to win concessions about Berlin, and possibly to secure the removal from England, Italy, and Turkey of 105 American intermediate-range ballistic missiles (45 Jupiter and 60 Thor weapons). Given this analysis, the committee concluded that the range of American responses included invasion, air attack, ultimatum, and blockade. President Kennedy decided that as a first step, Cuba should be blockaded.

On October 22, the president announced publicly that he would be seeking such an endorsement for a ''quarantine'' of all offensive weapon deliveries to Cuba that would start in two days' time. Kennedy also made it clear that a tighter watch would be kept over the island, that dependents (an eventual total of 3,190 people) would be evacuated from the U.S. Navy's base at Guantanamo Bay in the southeastern corner of Cuba, and that the Guantanamo Bay base would be reinforced by 8,000 men of the U.S. Marine Corps, who arrived by air and sea.

At the same time, President Kennedy let it be known through diplomatic channels that any attack on the continental United States by Cuban-based missiles would be regarded as an act of war by the Soviets and would thus call down on the U.S.S.R. the full weight of American nuclear retaliation. For the seaward defence of its Guantanamo Bay base, the U.S. Navy created Task Force 135, which included the aircraft carriers U.S.S. *Enterprise* and U.S.S. *Independence,* with nuclear and conventional propulsion arrangements respectively, and these two ships carried a formidable air complement of eight attack, four fighter, and two reconnaissance squadrons.

American Forces on Full Alert

Placed on full alert, the Strategic Air Command put its heavy bombers on 15-minute readiness. Some of the force was redeployed to civilian airports to reduce the chances of its being caught on its well-known bases, and a sizeable proportion of the force was kept airborne at all

The Cuban missile crisis was not confined to the United States' southern ''backyard,'' for the threat of war with the U.S.S.R. had global ramifications. These M48 battle tanks were from the American garrison in West Berlin, an obvious focal point for hostilities between the eastern and western blocs led respectively by the U.S.A. and the U.S.S.R.

Top: The Cuban missile crisis and the consequent worsening of American-Soviet relations was a considerable spur to the development of U.S. nuclear capabilities. This included the 31 nuclear-powered ballistic missile submarines of the "Lafayette" class, which is exemplified here by the U.S.S. *Nathan Hale*, sixth boat of the class. The "Lafayette" class was an enlarged version of the "Ethan Allen" class.

Bottom: By the time of the Cuban missile crisis, an increasing part of the U.S. nuclear deterrent capability was being carried by the navy's force of nuclear-powered ballistic missile submarines. Each of these boats carried 16 Polaris nuclear-tipped ballistic missiles as their primary offensive armament. The first five boats were the "George Washington" class, evolved from the "Skipjack" class of nuclear-powered attack submarines by the simple expedient of inserting a 130-foot (39·6-m) missile section aft of the sail. Seen here is the U.S.S. *Ethan Allen*, name boat of the navy's second nuclear-powered ballistic missile submarine class, which was also the first to be designed for this vital role.

times. It was also thought desirable to strengthen the air defenses of the southeastern states, and the local air-defense forces were swelled by Air-Defense Command and Tactical Air Command fighter squadrons, as well as HAWK and Nike surface-to-air missile battalions from less threatened parts of the United States.

The U.S. Navy also sent to sea as many of its nuclear-powered missile submarines as possible. If the U.S.S.R. tried to take advantage of the situation, the underwater-launched Polaris nuclear-tipped missiles on the submarines would

then be ready. The army's response was to strengthen its ground forces in the southeastern states by 30,000 men (including the 1st Armored Division) and more than 100,000 tons of equipment.

On October 23, the United States asked the Security Council of the United Nations to order the dismantling of Soviet missile installations in Cuba, and the Council of the Organization of American States approved a resolution authorizing the use of force to make the "quarantine" effective.

On the same day, the U.S.S.R. placed its forces on full alert and challenged the

43

An American reconnaissance photograph of the *Metallurg Anasov*, a Soviet freighter, revealed that she might be carrying eight surface-to-surface strategic missiles as deck cargo.

Below: The U.S.S. *Vesole*, a "Gearing" class fleet destroyer converted after World War II into an antisubmarine ocean escort, closes up alongside the Soviet Freighter *Volgoles* for a close inspection of the latter's deck cargo on November 9, 1962.

Right: A vertical reconnaissance photograph of November 10, 1962, reveals the site at La Coloma in Cuba where a major installation was being created for the SA- 2 ''Guideline'' surface-to-air missile.

Below: A further photograph of the surface-to-air missile site at La Coloma highlights the fact that operational missiles had already been installed on the launchers, and that reload missiles were present for rapid replenishment of used weapons.

right of the United States to blockade its shipments to Cuba. With the situation deteriorating rapidly toward the point of possible war between the superpowers, American planning for a possible invasion of Cuba, initially low-level, was put on a higher footing.

The ''quarantine'' of Cuba began early on October 25. As elements of the 2nd Fleet moved into the region where the blockade was to be enforced, hundreds of U.S. Air Force and U.S. Navy aircraft started a systematic search of the western Atlantic and the Caribbean for ships that might be carrying Soviet weapons. Reconnaissance of the missile sites on Cuba showed that construction was continuing without a pause. The world was very close to war as the two superpowers confronted each other directly over Cuba.

The tension was increased still further by the possibility of naval interception of any Soviet merchant ships that might be carrying offensive weapons to

Cuba. It later became clear, however, that the Soviets had no real taste for such brinksmanship and had ordered all their merchantmen to return home.

In the order signed on October 23, the ''quarantine'' zone originally envisaged a barrier about 800 miles from Cuba. This was later reduced to 500 miles so that the Soviets would have the time to radio instructions to their ships already in the zone. To police the zone, the U.S. Navy

created Task Force 136, which had 180 ships, including the antisubmarine carrier U.S.S. *Essex* with two squadrons of Grumman S-2A Tracker aircraft.

(On September 18, 1962, a tri-service rationalization of army, navy/marine corps, and air force equipment came into force so that the same basic designation system was used by the forces. The S-2A version of the Tracker piston-engined antisubmarine warplane had been the S2F-1 in the previous navy/marine corps system.)

As the "quarantine" went into effect, the three services continued their reconnaissance overflights of Cuba. In addition to the U-2s, which flew a total of 102 sorties at very high altitude during the crisis, the two types of aircraft used most extensively for reconnaissance duties were the RF-101C Voodoos of the U.S. Air Force's 29th Tactical Reconnaissance Squadron, and the Vought RF-8A Crusaders of the U.S. Navy's VFP-62 squadron and the U.S. Marine Corps' VMJC-2 squadron. At the same time, the navy and marine corps pressed ahead with their rapidly evolved plan to move tactical aircraft into the region of possible conflict: on October 20, the number of fighter, attack, and patrol aircraft available in this sector had been 109, 69, and

Another vertical reconnaissance photograph reveals an assembly site in Cuba for Soviet-supplied SA-2 "Guideline" surface-to-air missiles. The annotations highlight the site's major features.

30 respectively; by October 28, these totals had increased to 336, 218, and 78 respectively.

Typical of the reinforcement effort was that of the U.S. Marine Corps, which was primarily responsible for the land defense of the base at Guantanamo Bay. The base's original garrison had already been increased to regimental strength. The rest of the 2nd Marine Division, the marine component of the Atlantic Fleet, moved south into the Caribbean in amphibious warfare vessels. From the west coast assets of the Pacific Fleet's 1st Marine Division came the 5th Marine Expeditionary Brigade, which moved in amphibious warfare vessels via the Panama Canal into the Gulf of Mexico. The other major marine group that moved into the crisis sector was the east coast-based 2nd Marine Air Wing, which deployed into Florida and Puerto Rico.

Secret Negotiations Bear Fruit

Even as the U.S. forces gathered, however, President Kennedy and Premier Khrushchev had been in secret negotiation since October 24 in an effort to defuse the situation. In an exchange of

letters, the American president warned of the dangers should the U.S.S.R. continue its policy of exerting pressure on the United States, and on October 26, the Soviet premier indicated that the U.S.S.R. would back down, writing in a letter which Kennedy accepted on October 28 that the Soviets would halt all construction work associated with offensive weapons, and then dismantle and remove these weapons from Cuba. At this time, the medium- and intermediate-range ballistic missiles that had triggered the crisis were being supplemented by 44 Ilyushin Il-28 ''Beagle'' light bombers that were being assembled at San Julian. Khrushchev's only major condition was that the U.S. withdraw its Jupiter missiles from Europe, a decision that Kennedy had already

Above Right: One of the Soviet aircraft types supplied to Cuba was the Ilyushin Il-28 ''Beagle'' jet-powered light bomber. This type was obsolescent by the latest standards, but was capable of delivering a nuclear bombload into the southern states.

Right: While vertical photography is highly important in aerial reconnaissance, oblique shots can provide a more graphic image, as indicated by this low-level photograph of San Julian airfield on October 27, 1962, with Ilyushin Il-62 ''Beagle'' light bombers being assembled.

UNCRATED FUSELAGE AND TAIL SECTION

BEAGLES BEING ASSEMBLED

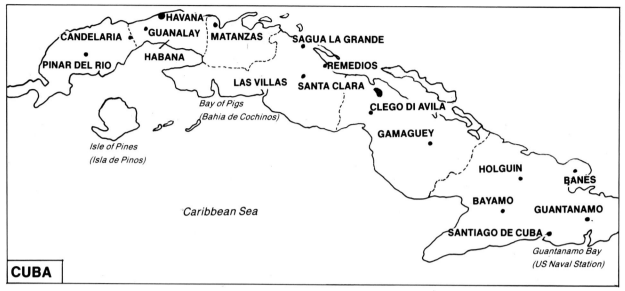

CUBA

Cuba: the communist thorn in the United States southern flank.

taken. Kennedy also agreed that the U.S. "quarantine" of Cuba would be lifted as soon as the United Nations reported that Soviet offensive weapons had been removed, and he pledged that the United States would not mount any invasion of Cuba.

As the two leaders were negotiating, the tension flared still higher because of two separate incidents involving U-2 reconnaissance aircraft. On October 27, Major Rudolph Anderson of the 29th Tactical Reconnaissance Squadron was killed during a reconnaissance sortie over the Cuban naval installation at Banes: an SA-2 missile exploded near his U-2E, rupturing the pressure suit that allowed Anderson to survive at the airplane's very high cruising altitude. On October 28, the Soviets put their intercontinental ballistic missile force on alert after another U-2 strayed from its planned course and overflew the Chutostkiy Peninsula on the eastern tip of Siberia.

The Crisis is Defused

The crisis began to wind down on October 28 as the two sides agreed on the dismantling of the Soviet missiles in Cuba under the supervision of the United Nations Organization. The merchant ship *Dvinogorsk* departed from Mariel on November 5 with four SS-4 missiles; another eight missiles were shipped out on November 7 on the *Metali... Anosov*, and a further six left on November 9 on board the *Bratsk*. Yet the Il-28 bombers were still under construction at San Julian, and the U.S. "quarantine" of Cuba did not end until November 20, when the Soviets finally agreed to remove these potentially dangerous and thus provocative aircraft. The Il-28 were steadily dismantled, and the first of them left Cuba during December 15 on board the *Kasimov*.

Throughout this period, the American forces maintained their aerial surveillance of Cuba with high-flying U-2Es and the lower-flying combination of RF-8As and RF-101Cs to make sure that the Soviets complied with their half of the bargain struck between Kennedy and Khrushchev, and that the deactivated missile sites remained inactive. The relaxation of tension during November allowed a number of forces that had been shifted to the Southeast to return to their bases, but it was only in the days just before Christmas 1962 that the last forces were stood down.

The crisis officially ended on January 7, 1963, when the United States and U.S.S.R. reported to U Thant, the Secretary-General of the United Nations Organization, that their dispute over Cuba was over. Yet there was still congressional concern that the Soviets might not have fulfilled their half of the bargain fully, and it was only on February 6 that Secretary of Defense Robert S. McNamara was able to convince Congress, with the aid of aerial reconnaissance photographs, that all Soviet offensive weapons had left the island. But even though the Soviet offensive weapons had gone, a large number of Soviet personnel remained in Cuba, and on May 9, the Department of defense calculated that they totaled 17,500 men, including 5,000 combat troops.

Positive Results of the Cuban Missile Crisis

The crisis had emphasized the fact that the threat of global war made a better and faster means of communication necessary than was currently available to the two superpower leaders. As a result, a direct line connecting the two leaders was inaugurated on August 30, 1963; the so-called "hot line" between the White House in Washington and the Kremlin in Moscow. Further evidence of eased relations between the United States and the U.S.S.R. came on August 5, 1963, when the two countries signed the Partial Test-Ban Treaty prohibiting nuclear weapon tests in the atmosphere, in space, and underwater.

As a postscript to the Cuban Missile Crisis, Cuba was still unhappy with the presence of the U.S. naval base at Guantanamo Bay, and on February 6, 1964, the Cubans cut the water supply to the base. However, the availability of a distillation plant made the base independent of Cuban water.

Soviet ballistic missiles launched from Cuba could plunge deep into the United States.

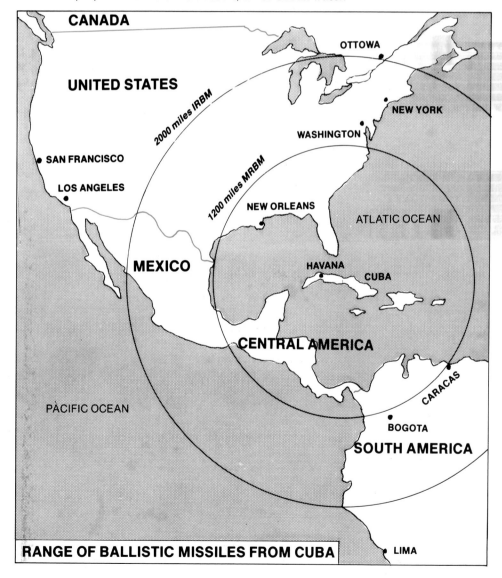

RANGE OF BALLISTIC MISSILES FROM CUBA

Intervention in the Dominican Republic (1965)

Throughout the 1950s and 1960s, Europe and Asia remained the main strategic preoccupations of the United States. However, the "defection" of Cuba to the communist bloc and the Cuban Missile Crisis were nasty reminders that events closer to home could have an unfortunate effect on the United States if they were not checked. From the early 1960s, therefore, the U.S. defense establishment started to pay closer attention to events in the country's Caribbean "backyard." There were many volatile points, none more so than the island of Hispaniola just east of Cuba, where the countries of Haiti and the Dominican Republic occupied the western one-third and eastern two-thirds of the island.

The Dominican Republic had existed with a measure of long-term stability under the dictatorship of Leonidas Trujillo, but this 31-year period ended in May 1961 with Trujillo's assassination. On September 25, 1963, a left-wing government headed by Juan Bosch was overthrown by the Dominican military forces, but in October the government was restored to civilian hands in the form of a political triumvirate. On April 24, 1965, another military rebellion broke out, and after the civilian government had been overthrown, a bloody civil war erupted though the streets of Santo Domingo, capital of the Dominican Republic.

As the safety of American nationals was in question, President Lyndon B. Johnson ordered the U.S. Marine Corps to carry out the safe evacuation of these civilians. The helicopter-carrying amphibious assault ship U.S.S. *Boxer* was ordered into the area with the 6th Marine Expeditionary Unit, whose two main assets were Battalion Landing Team 3/6

The Dominican intervention made great demands on the ability of the U.S. Marine Corps to respond rapidly with significant strength. Seen here on the deck of the U.S.S. *Boxer*, are two of the corps' major helicopter types, the Sikorsky CH-37 heavy and Bell UH-1 light helicopters. The twin-engined CH-37 had main landing-gear units that retracted into the engine nacelles, and its clamshell nose allowed the craft to carry a light vehicle as part of its internal load.

Left: Men of the 568th Engineer Battalion instruct personnel of the Dominican Army's engineer battalion in the art of building a floating bridge. This one was installed during June 1966 as a temporary replacement for the President Troncoso Bridge, which had been washed out after heavy rains.

Below: An aerial view of the Ambassador Hotel and its environs in Santo Domingo during the Dominican crisis reveals evidence of the U.S. intervention; the parked trucks, other vehicles, tents, and the entrance to a bunker can all be seen.

Left: A pair of McDonnell RF-101 Voodoo aircraft departs Ramey Air Force Base in Puerto Rico on a tactical reconnaissance mission over the Dominican Republic during May 1965.

Below: An M50 Ontos antitank vehicle of the U.S. Marine Corps guards a tactically important position in May 1965.

(the 3rd Battalion of the 6th Marine Regiment) and the HMM-264 squadron with medium transport helicopters. The situation in Santo Domingo deteriorated rapidly, and the loyalist forces were soon unable to guarantee the safety of either the American embassy or the designated evacuation site. The loyalists asked for a U.S. battalion to stabilize the local situation, and the 3rd Battalion of the 6th Marine Regiment was helicoptered ashore on April 29 to occupy and hold the western part of Santo Domingo.

As the crisis had started, the 82nd Airborne Division had been put on alert at its base at Fort Bragg, North Carolina. Less than 72 hours later, the division was ordered to send two of its battalions by tactical air transport to seize the airfield east of Santo Domingo. The airborne soldiers accomplished this task without much difficulty on April 30, and soon another four battalions and some support elements had also arrived. Command of the U.S. forces was assumed by Lieutenant General Bruce Palmer, Jr., who decided that the best way to separate the warring Dominican factions was to drive an east/west American corridor through the city, thereby dividing the two factional forces, whose main units held the north and south of the city. The operation was carried out at night using three airborne battalions: the first started the operation, and the other two then passed through this battalion to link up with the marines. The operation proceeded without difficulty, and Palmer then expanded this corridor into an International Safety Zone.

Santo Domingo

For further references see pages 50, *55*, 56, 57, *58*, *59*, *60*, 61

An aerial view of the control and reporting center established by the Americans at the San Isidro Air Base during the Dominican intervention. The main part of the base was a major supply depot.

Opposite Top Left: As always happens in an intervention into the affairs of another country, U.S. forces were caught between the opposing factions. Thus any decision that seemed to favor one side was immediately used by the other side as the basis for grievance and protest. This women's protest took place outside the Ambassador Hotel on May 25, 1965.

Opposite Top Right: The banner of the Dominican communist party, complete with a portrait of Lenin, is carried past the U.S. Embassy in Santo Domingo during a protest march on April 28, 1966, the first anniversary of the U.S. intervention.

Opposite Bottom Left: The size of the Sikorsky CH-37's hold is neatly revealed in this photograph of the helicopter's clamshell doors and an all-purpose Mule vehicle with a load of water containers.

Above: Dominican civilians cluster around a U.S. Marine Corps' Sikorsky CH-34 helicopter which had flown food and medicine into a village hard hit by Hurricane ''Inez'' during October 1966.

Left: Men of the 2nd Special Forces (Airborne Infantry) learn the use of a double-rope bridge during basic antiguerrilla training at Camp Hutchinson outside Santo Domingo during July 1966. The camp was operated by the 1st Battalion, 504th Parachute Infantry Regiment, 82nd Airborne Division.

Above: Men of the 82nd Airborne Division man a 106-mm (4·17-inch) recoilless rifle mounted on a jeep at the edge of the safety zone around a rebel-held area of Santo Domingo during May 7/8, 1965.

By the end of the first week in May, the United States had moved all nine battalions of the 82nd Airborne Division into Santo Domingo. Another two marine battalions, the 1st Battalions of the 6th and 8th Marine Regiments, were delivered by air, and a local reserve was provided by the 1st Battalion of the 2nd Marine Regiment, which remained offshore in the helicopter assault ship U.S.S. *Okinawa.*

With support elements, U.S. forces totaled 23,000 men. They patrolled Santo Domingo as a temporary police force to maintain law and order, and tried to ease the local situation by distributing food, water, and medicine to each side without partiality. The rapid arrival of the American force was largely instrumental in halting the fighting, and the size to which it soon grew made it impractical to resume hostilities. In this stalemated situation,

Above: U.S. Marines and their M50 Ontos light antitank vehicle lurk by the remnants of a demolished building during fighting with Dominican rebels on May 15, 1965.

The Commander's Summary of operations in the Dominican Republic provided the reasons for intervention. It is notable that the leader received both public and secret instructions:

Decision to Intervene, Mission, and Size of US Force:

1. a. *President Johnson's decision to intervene was made on 27 April 1965, based on urgent reports of US Ambassador Bennett that:*

> *(1) Situation was out of control.*
> *(2) US lives and property were endangered.*
> *(3) Junta could not handle and had asked for US help.*
> *(4) There was danger of a communist takeover.*

b. *US Marines, BLT 3/6 (Battalion landing team) landed at Red Beach near Haina on 28 April and immediately secured US Embassy and the Hotel Embajador (safe haven for all evacuees, US and others).*

c. *President committed additional US forces – Marines and Army on 29-30 April. He also designated Lt Gen Palmer, US Army, by name to command the forces ashore. At his Pentagon office, General Wheeler, Chairman Joint Chiefs of Staff, informed Lt Gen Palmer, of the above with the following additional instructions:*

2. *Your announced mission is to save US lives. Your unstated mission is to prevent the Dominican Republic from going communist. The President has stated that he will not allow another Cuba – you are to take all necessary measures required to accomplish this mission. You will be given sufficient forces to do the job.*

The operation progressed. It provided lessons relevant to the Panama mission of 1989-90.

Shortly after midnight Gen Palmer arrived with a small staff to assume command of all land forces in the DOM REP. On 1 May Gen Palmer's concern for a secure route through Santo Domingo by which to evacuate US nationals dictated dispatch of a remon patrol to link-up with the Marine elements. This patrol which had

seven casualties – 2 KIA, 5 WIA – made link-up at 1245 hours and confirmed the presence of a strong rebel force within the area which would eventually become the corridor. Based on this patrol action, authority was granted on 2 May to open a corridor.

Phase II of our operation was the opening and expanding of the corridor. This operation commenced just after midnight on 2 May and was complete in one hour and 14 minutes against very modest resistance. The decision to execute in the middle of the night was made to attempt surprise, avoid civilian casualties, and hopefully to pass forces along the route and hold at daylight. The wisdom of this decision was soon confirmed. The extreme importance of accurate and complete intelligence is spotlighted by this operation. Had the senior ground commanders known more about the situation at this time and had our intelligence on utility installations been more complete, we could have seized radio Santo Domingo and the main water valves in Northern Santo Domingo, both of which were two blocks outside our corridor. Had we included the radio station in our corridor we could have avoided many future headaches and had a significant lever to use on the rebels. This is something the intelligence community and commanders should be aware of in future operations of this type.

Above: Men of the 82nd Airborne Division keep an easy but watchful eye on a pair of Dominican civilians after a firefight with rebels in Santo Domingo during May 10, 1965.

Right: The situation in the Dominican Republic eased considerably after the American intervention force was supplemented and then partially replaced by troops from Central and South American states. This is a convoy of Honduran soldiers arriving at their base on May 20, 1965.

Above: A detachment of the 82nd Airborne Division holds one of the dividing lines between government and rebel areas of Santo Domingo on May 10, 1965.

Left: Cautious soldiers of the 82nd Airborne Division keep themselves ready for action after a firefight in Santo Domingo during May 10, 1965.

Above: An American patrol rounds up rebel suspects during an operation to pacify part of Santo Domingo on May 11, 1965.

Right: U.S. forces were involved in retraining the Dominican Army. In this photograph of early 1970, men of the Airborne Special Forces attached to the U.S. Military Assistance Advisory Group demonstrate the technique of landing after a parachute drop, and then bundling the parachute to prevent the wind from catching it and pulling the landed man along the ground.

the two Dominican factions settled down to negotiations that lasted into September.

Internal and External Opposition

Despite its success and lack of significant bloodshed, the American intervention produced considerable opposition within the United States and in other nations in the western hemisphere. The Organization of American States was asked to take a hand in the matter. Despite the disagreement of several Latin American countries, the Organization of American States decided to create a multinational peacekeeping force that eventually included contingents from Brazil, Costa Rica, El Salvador, Honduras, Nicaragua, and Paraguay in addition to that of the United States, the first ever inter-American force.

These contingents began to arrive in

Right: Soldiers of the U.S. Military Assistance Advisory Group teach Dominican troops of the 1st Battalion, 1st Infantry Brigade, how to operate the M60 machine gun.

Below: Dominican infantrymen of the 3rd Battalion, 1st Infantry Brigade, wade across a small river near Fort Aleza under the watchful eyes of their American advisers.

Santo Domingo in May, and although the U.S. force was by far the largest and most effective, political considerations demanded a non-American commander. Palmer therefore became second-in-command to a Brazilian officer, Lieutenant General Hugo Panasco Alvim, late in May. With the arrival of the Central and South American contingents, U.S. units were gradually withdrawn. The marines had departed by June, and tension was further eased in September, when both Dominican factions accepted a provisional government. The U.S. Army force was steadily reduced to three battalions by the end of the year. Together with the Central and South American contingents, the last United States troops departed in the middle of 1966 after successful Dominican elections. The occupation had lasted for 16 months, and although there were serious questions about the legality of the initial American effort, there can be no doubt that in practical terms it prevented considerable bloodshed.

Above Left: Men of the Dominican Army's 1st Battalion, 1st Infantry Brigade, undergo gas-mask training while learning the arts of riot control at 25 Kilo Camp.

Above Right: As part of their riot-control training at 25 Kilo Camp, Dominican soldiers were faced with the difficult task of attempting to disperse demonstrators during a simulated protest rally.

Right: The arts of local camouflage are tested by men of the Dominican Army's 3rd Battalion, 1st Infantry Brigade, during training at Fort Aleza.

Civil Strife in the United States
(1950s and 1960s)

One of the most difficult and morale-sapping tasks of troops in the continental United States during the late 1960s and early 1970s was the maintenance of order in areas riven by riot or lesser forms of civil disorder. This inevitably brought anger and hatred down on the forces, reflected in episodes such as the incident illustrated here, the burning of the ROTC building at Kent State University, Ohio, on May 2, 1970.

Even before these events had begun to develop in the Caribbean, racial tensions were developing within the United States as an offshoot of the civil rights movement. A crop of civil disturbances resulted, and the manner and scale of the use of troops reminded many people of the government's use of troops in the labor disputes of the late 1800s.

The first, and probably the most dramatic, of these events took place in September 1957, when there was serious doubt that nine black students would be able to take advantage of a court order permitting them to attend the previously all-white Central High School in Little Rock, Arkansas. President Eisenhower despatched a complete battle group of the 101st Airborne Division and brought into federal service the complete Arkansas National Guard. The airborne soldiers broke up the mob outside the school and,

over the next few weeks, maintained order in Little Rock before delegating responsibility to the Arkansas National Guard. For the rest of the school year, the National Guard maintained a force of about 400 men on the task.

It was the first time since 1867 that a president had used his power to call militia forces into federal service to control an internal matter, and it was also one of the few episodes in American history when the president used federal forces (either regular troops or federalized militia) for a task opposed by a state governor.

The Little Rock episode was followed by a number of similar events during the Kennedy and Johnson presidencies. When, for example, the governor of Mississippi attempted to prevent the legally mandated registration of a black student at the University of Mississippi in Oxford, President Kennedy tried to use federal marshals to enforce the law. On the night after the black student's registration, however, rioting broke out on the university campus, and the federal marshals were too few in number to break up the disturbance. The president then

Lyndon B. Johnson

For further references
see pages
50, 57, 63, 6124

Two of the greatest
advocates of full civil
rights for minorities
during the 1960s were
President Lyndon B.
Johnson and Dr.
Martin Luther King,
seen here on May 8,
1965, as he arrived for
a meeting with the
president.

called the Mississippi National Guard into federal service and ordered regular army units to move into Oxford from their holding areas in Memphis, Tennessee. So great was the problem that 30,000 men (20,000 regular soldiers and 10,000 federalized national guardsmen) were involved: 12,000 men in Oxford and the other 18,000 on standby in the area. Once the military gained control of the situation, the tension eased and the troops were gradually pulled out, although some men were retained in Oxford until the end of the academic year.

A similar course of events occurred during 1963 in Alabama, where the governor refused to implement desegregation orders. President Kennedy again ordered in regular army troops, and he called the Alabama National Guard into federal service. In 1965, President Johnson used both types of forces to protect a civil rights march from Selma to Montgomery.

By this time, though, the emphasis in racial matters was switching from the south, where the nature of civil rights was the most important issue, to the major cities of the north, where blacks had become increasingly unhappy with the slum conditions in which they lived. This stage of protest was therefore as much

economic as political, and it found its most dangerous form in rioting, looting, and arson. The worst of these episodes was the huge 1965 riot in the predominantly black area of Watts in Los Angeles. The governor called out some 13,400 men of the California National Guard in the protracted effort to curb the rioting, prevent the looting, extinguish the fires, and then restore the rule of law.

The Watts episode was a harbinger of events in the following two years. In the summer of 1967, there were major riots in more than ten American cities, including Detroit, where there was virtually complete anarchy for almost a week. In an initial attempt to restore order, the governor called in 8,000 men of the Michigan National Guard to assist the local police. These forces were too small for the job at hand, and for the first time in almost a quarter of a century, a state governor requested federal troops. President Johnson responded by sending in units of the 82nd and 101st Airborne Divisions, and by calling the Michigan National Guard into federal service for subordination to army command. The combined forces of the police, National Guard, and army finally restored peace, though only at the cost of some bloodshed.

The *Mayaguez* Rescue
(1975)

Of all the military operations undertaken by the U.S. forces in the 20th century, few have divided the American public as strongly as the April 1970 invasion of Cambodia ordered by President Richard M. Nixon. Despite its supposed neutrality, the Cambodia ruled by the communist Prince Norodom Sihanouk had become a haven for North Vietnamese and Viet Cong forces operating in South Vietnam. Occupying much of the Cambodia's eastern region, the communist forces received an increasing quantity of equipment and other supplies from North Vietnam via the southbound Ho Chi Minh Trail, and from other communist countries via the so-called Sihanouk Trail, which stretched north from the port of Kompong Som on the Cambodian coast.

Eventually tiring of the use of his country by foreign communists, Sihanouk traveled to Moscow to remonstrate with the communist leadership. In his absence, he was overthrown in October 1970 and replaced by the military government of Lieutenant General Lon Nol, who renamed the country the Khmer Republic. Lon Nol's forces held the main cities of the Khmer Republic, but about 60 percent of the country's land area was soon controlled by Khmer Rouge communist forces loyal to Sihanouk. A bitter civil war followed, and despite last-minute U.S. assistance to Lon Nol, the communists finally triumphed. They took Phnom Penh, the capital, on April 17, 1975, just as the long Vietnam War was also drawing to a close: a complete communist victory.

On May 12, 1975, less than two weeks after the fall of Saigon and the end of the Vietnam War, Khmer forces seized the SS *Mayaguez*, an American-registered ship built in World War II. The vessel had been revised as a 10,485-ton container ship and plied a regular route between Hong Kong and Singapore, with an intermediate stop at the Thai port of Sattahip. The ship belonged to Sea-Land Services,

Khmer Rouge
For further references see pages 66, 67, 68, 69, 70, *71*

Inc., and had two cranes to handle her cargo of 35-foot containers, of which 274 could be carried.

While steaming in international waters some 68 miles southwest of the Cambodian coast, but only 6½ miles from the most southern of the Khmer Republic's Poulo Wai Islands, the ship was approached by Khmer patrol boats, ironically American-built Swift boats supplied to Lon Nol's forces, but now in service with the Khmer Rouge. One of these boats fired a shot across the *Mayaguez*'s bows to halt the ship and then put a party aboard to seize the vessel. As the situation developed, the *Mayaguez*'s radio operator had broadcast details of the ship's plight, so the event came rapidly to the attention of the American authorities as the boarding party ordered the ship into Khmer territorial waters.

The situation in this area was extremely sensitive in the aftermath of the Vietnam War. General David C. Jones, acting chairman of the Joint Chiefs of Staff in the absence of General George Brown, who was on a routine European tour, made sure that he had the express authority of Secretary of Defense James Schlesinger before sending any U.S. forces into the area. With this authority provided by his political superior, Jones ordered Admiral Noel Gayler, commander-in-chief of Pacific Command, to send reconnaissance aircraft to locate the missing ship. It was only after this process had begun that President Gerald R. Ford learned of events and gave his full support to the military activities that were now being set in motion.

In the morning of May 13, a Lockheed P-3 Orion of a U.S. Navy squadron based in Thailand spotted the *Mayaguez* in the Poulo Wai Islands. Shortly afterward, the ship was anchored off Koh Tang Island, and on the following day, the ship's 40-man crew was moved to nearby Koah Rong Sam Loem Island. This and further information was gleaned by the P-3 as well as a number of General Dynamics F-111 aircraft sent in by the U.S. Air Force, commanded by Lieutenant General John J. Burns. With all the relevant data in their hands, the Joint Chiefs of Staff and the National Security Council recommended to President Ford that a rescue

The greatest American warplane of the 1960s, and one of the finest combat aircraft of all time, was the McDonnell F-4 Phantom II. It was produced in response to the navy's requirement for a fighter able to provide area air defense of the fleet at a considerable range from its parent carrier. The fighter was therefore a two-seater with powerful radar and a large complement of air-to-air missiles. The craft had initially been projected as a carrierborne attack fighter, and these origins came full circle as the Phantom II evolved into a magnificent multirole fighter able to undertake the fighter, attack, and strike roles with steadily more powerful engines and radar. So successful was the plane in service with the navy and marine corps that, in a highly unusual move, it was adopted by the air force as a land-based multirole warplane. Further improvements were centered on electronic enhancement, increased agility, and improved combat capability through the development of variants with inbuilt cannon armament for short-range engagements during dogfights.

attempt should be undertaken. Despite the fact that the area was a political minefield, the president felt that the United States had to rebuild its credibility after the Vietnam War with a small but decisive action. One such as this would also serve to discourage other acts of politically inspired piracy.

The Forces Gather

The phased withdrawal from Thailand of U.S. forces involved in the air war in Vietnam had been ordered two months earlier, but was still in its early stages. This meant that there were substantial American air and naval assets available locally. Planning could begin for a rescue launched as quickly as possible, so that the Khmer Rouge forces had little time for defensive preparations. The American forces in Thailand lacked only the right

type of troops for the operation, so 430 men of the 3rd Marine Division were flown in by Lockheed C-141A StarLifter transports of the U.S. Air Force's Military Airlift Command: Company "D" of the 1st Battalion, 4th Marine Regiment, arrived from Subic Bay in the Philippines, and Battalion Landing Team 2/9 (the 2nd Battalion of the 9th Marine Regiment) from Okinawa. A carrier battle group was also alerted to support the operation after moving into the Gulf of Siam, including the aircraft carrier U.S.S. *Coral Sea*, the missile cruiser U.S.S. *Gridley*, the destroyer U.S.S. *Bausell*, and the deastroyer escort U.S.S. *Iang*.

A Launch Point in Thailand

The rescue effort was to be mounted from U-Tapao in southern Thailand, despite protests from the Thai government.

Although the operation was planned around only a small force of troops, considerable air assets were gathered in an interesting commentary on the size and versatility of the American air forces at this time. These warplanes included the Vought A-7D attack aircraft of the 388th Tactical Fighter Wing, the McDonnell Douglas F-4E multirole fighters of the 432nd Tactical Fighter Wing, the General Dynamics F-111A interdictors of the 347th Tactical Fighter Wing, the Lockheed C-130E Hercules transports of the 374th Tactical Airlift Wing, the Lockheed AC-130E Hercules gunships of the 16th Special Operations Squadron, the Lockheed HC-130P Hercules tanker and recovery aircraft of the 56th Aerospace Rescue & Recovery Squadron, the Sikorsky HH-53C Super Jolly combat rescue helicopters of the 40th Aerospace Rescue & Recovery Squadron, and the Sikorsky CH-53C transport helicopters of the 21st Special Operations Squadron. These land-based aircraft were complemented by the Grumman A-6A Intruder and Vought A-7E Corsair II attack warplanes, supported by McDonnell Douglas F-4N Phantom II fighters, of the *Coral Sea*s Carrier Air Wing 15.

The U.S. forces suffered their first losses of the operation during this buildup, when a CH-53C crashed on transit from Nakhon Phanom to U-Tapao, killing five airmen and 18 air policemen. The first warplane to see action was an AC-130E gunship. During the night of May 13-14, it was maintaining a surveillance of Khmer Rouge craft operating between *Mayaguez* and Koh Tang Island, and was fired on by Khmer Rouge gunboats and light antiaircraft guns. Later in the morning, U.S. warplanes took limited offensive action when an AC-130E fired warning shots across the bow of a Khmer Rouge patrol boat in an effort to prevent the movement of the *Mayaguez*'s crew to the mainland. Later the same day, fighters fired warning shots at Khmer Rouge craft and fishing vessels, sinking five of the craft and severely damaging another two. The warplanes also dropped riot-control gas. Even so, the Khmer Rouge forces were able to move the crew of the *Mayaguez* off Koh Tang Island without alerting the

The global reach of the U.S. forces in recent times has been based to a large extent on naval power and the use of prepositioned equipment. However, the support of forces deployed far from home is greatly dependent on heavy air transportation using two Lockheed aircraft, the C-141 StarLifter and the C-5 Galaxy. The plane illustrated here is the StarLifter, which was designed as a logistic transport capable of undertaking the long-range strategic airlift role. The plane is of the classic military transport configuration pioneered by the turboprop-powered Lockheed C-130 Hercules in the early 1950s. Its high-set wing and external blister fairings for the main landing gear units leave the fuselage unobstructed for its primary transportation function. Access to the hold is provided by a clamshell rear ramp/door arrangement under the upswept tail, a design that simplifies the task of loading and unloading bulky and/or long items of freight.

suspicions of the Americans. By this time, the rescue operation itself was beginning to get underway as the helicopters transporting the assault troops prepared to leave U-Tapao.

The Rescue Mission Starts

Early in the morning of May 15, Phnom Penh radio indicated the Khmer Rouge authorities might consider the release of the *Mayaguez*, but made no mention of the ship's American crewmen. It was decided to begin the rescue operation, therefore, and before first light, six HH-53C and five CH-53C helicopters set off from U-Tapao, their holds filled with marines. Three of the HH-53Cs made a rendezvous with the destroyer escort U.S.S. *Harold E. Holt* and transferred the marines of Company "D," 1st Battalion, 4th Marine Regiment, who were to board and recapture the *Mayaguez*. The other eight helicopters continued on their way to Koh Tang Island with 131 marines of Battalion Landing Team 2/9.

The task of the boarding party was simple. The destroyer escort reached the *Mayaguez* and found her abandoned. The marines boarded the container ship, which was soon taken under tow for movement into international waters.

The task of the party that landed on Koh Tang Island was far harder and

resulted in a 14-hour action that was ultimately pointless, as the crew of the *Mayaguez* had already been moved. Under the command of Lieutenant Colonel Randall W. Austin, the marines landed on the northern promontory of the island in two groups: the larger landed on a beach on the western side of this tip, which is 370 yards wide, and the smaller on a beach on the eastern side, which was connected with the western beach by a rough corridor about 110 yards wide which the Khmer Rouge had cleared through the jungle. The American plan was based on the assessment that the marines would have at least two-to-one numerical superiority over the Khmer Rouge garrison and the benefits of powerful tactical air support. The two forces were meant to advance inland from their landing beaches, link up, and cut off the northern tip of the island, where the crewmen of the *Mayaguez* were (erroneously) thought to be held.

Unexpectedly Heavy Fire

As they approached the western beach, the two leading helicopters were met by unexpectedly heavy small arms, rocket, and mortar fire. Both helicopters managed to unload their marines. One was hit; it managed a single-engine take-off, but soon had to ditch in the sea with

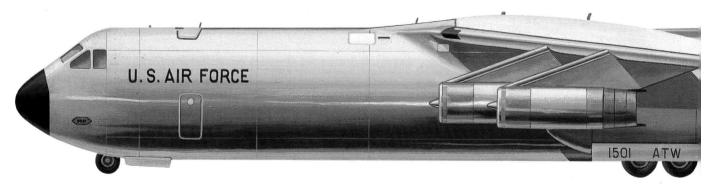

the loss of one crewman, while the other was struck in the fuel tanks and only just managed to make it back to the Thai coast before making an emergency landing. As the other helicopters approached to land men on the western beach, a third CH-53C helicopter was hit repeatedly, but managed to take off and return to Thailand with a seriously wounded man before making an emergency landing. In the western beach landing, therefore, the American force had lost three valuable helicopters.

The western landing had gone badly; the eastern landing fared even worse. Two of the CH-53Cs were shot down; the crew and marines of one escaped from their machine, but were pinned down on the beach by Khmer Rouge fire, and 13 men were killed when the other craft crashed. The two landings had thus succeeded in landing only 54 men in two separated groups on the island, and losses in men and materiel had been heavy. Up to this time, the American tactical aircraft in the area had not intervened for fear of hitting the marines on their two small "beach-heads." However, a survivor from one of the crashed helicopters on the eastern beach was a marine forward air con-

troller, and he was now able to coordinate air attacks that soon began to reduce the ability of the Khmer Rouge to pin down the marines on the island. As the fighters kept the Khmer Rouge gunners occupied, three HH-53Cs arrived to land more men on the western beach. One helicopter was driven off by Khmer Rouge antiaircraft fire, another landed its marine "grunts" in the right place, and the third deposited its men on a beach south of the one designated.

A Critical Position

Despite the arrival of these reinforcements, the American position on Koh Tang Island remained critical, because the 124 men were divided into three groups: 60 marines on the western beach, 29 marines south of the western beach, and 20 marines plus five air force personnel on the eastern beach. The three groups were unable to link up, and it was decided to evacuate the force on the eastern beach using one of the HH-53C's that had transferred the marines to the *Holt*. It had taken on fuel from an HC-130P and was now operating in the

search-and-rescue role. The attempt to lift the marines off the eastern beach had to be abandoned, however, when the helicopter was severely damaged.

As the men on the island tried again to join forces under cover of A-7D attack warplanes and AC-130E gunships, the aircraft of Carrier Air Wing 15 launched an attack against the Khmer Rouge airfield at Ream and destroyed 17 aircraft, 12 of them North American T-28D piston-engine light attack aircraft supplied to Cambodia in friendlier times. An hour later, a second attack destroyed the oil depot near Kompong Som. At much the same time, the 43rd Bombardment Wing at Andersen Air Force Base on Guam readied 15 Boeing B-52D Stratofortress heavy bombers with conventional "iron" bombs for a possible tactical strike if the position on Koh Tang Island did not improve.

Over the island itself, an A-7D served as a forward air controller for other A-7Ds that attacked Khmer Rouge positions, as an AC-130E used its side-firing combination of 20-mm cannon, 40-mm Bofors gun, and 105-mm (4·13-inch) howitzer to batter Khmer Rouge positions as close as 50 yards to the marines. This allowed an HH-53C to run in and land another party of marines, but by this time eight of the 11 helicopters that had been available at the start of the operation had been shot down or damaged so severely that they were unable to play a further part in the action.

The *Mayaguez*'s Crew is Returned

Fortunately for the success of the operation as a whole, later that morning, the missile destroyer U.S.S. *Henry B. Wilson* spotted the approach of a Thai fishing boat which the Khmer Rouge had commandeered to surrender the crew of the *Mayaguez*. The destroyer escort intercepted the boat, and in 22 minutes the American sailors had been transferred to the warship. In this providential manner, the second objective of the operation was achieved.

The task now facing the American commanders (General Burns in overall command and Colonel J. Anders in tactical command from an orbiting Lockheed EC-130E Hercules aerial command post) was to extract the marines on Koh Tang Is-

land. First, marines had to be landed to effect an overland rescue of the party stranded on the eastern beach. Here the Americans were fortunate; three helicopters (two CH-53Cs and one HH-53C) that had been unserviceable at the operation's beginning were now available.

One of the CH-53Cs was used in another effort to land men directly onto the beach, but it was defeated by heavy and accurate Khmer Rouge fire, which hit the helicopter in several places and forced it to break away without delivering its load. On the western beach, three HH-53Cs landed 108 marines and virtually doubled the marine strength on Koh Tang Island. The marine position on the western beach was strengthened further when the men of the isolated pocket to the south finally reached the main force to create a consolidated western force. Even so, formidable obstacles to the link-up of the western and eastern beach forces remained. Where there was not heavy jungle, the intervening land was littered with tree stumps and held in significant strength by the Khmer Rouge garrison.

Further Helicopter Losses

The plan adopted by the Americans was for tactical air power and the marines on the western beach to pin down the Khmer Rouge forces, thus creating a "window of opportunity" for helicopters to dash in and rescue the 25 men on the eastern beach. The first attempt to evacuate the men on the eastern beach was supported by A-7D warplanes, which dropped canisters of riot-control gas, but failed when one of the two HH-53Cs was struck by antiaircraft fire. The machine lost one of its two engines and had a fuel line punctured, so it only just reached the *Coral Sea*, which was now just 70 miles from the island.

It was clear that a successful helicopter operation demanded better close air support, so the air force dispatched two Rockwell OV-10A Bronco aircraft of the 23rd Tactical Air Support Squadron to spot targets and mark them for the tactical warplanes, which now included A-7Ds, F-4Es, and AC-130Es. The efforts of these warplanes combined with the gunfire of the *Henry B. Wilson* silenced many Khmer Rouge positions, but the marine's position was still extremely precarious as dusk approached.

At this time, the main body on the western beach had advanced about halfway across the neck of land separating it from the smaller cut-off force on the eastern beach. Its senior officer now realized that his men could not hope to reach the other force before nightfall. These 20 marines and five airmen had been isolated for ten hours, and a maximum effort was now made to extract them. One CH-53C and two HH-53Cs were despatched as tactical warplanes, gunships, and even the *Henry B. Wilson*'s longboat laid down suppressive fire. At the last minute, a C-130E transport dropped one 15,000-pound blast bomb on the Khmer Rouge positions, and as the defenders struggled to recover from the concussive effect of this weapon, one HH-53C dashed in and recovered all 25 men. The helicopter headed straight to the *Coral Sea* so that the wounded men could receive prompt medical attention.

The Last Men Are Evacuated

While searching in vain for survivors from a downed CH-53C, one of the surviving HH-53Cs received heavy damage and only just managed to stagger back to the *Coral Sea*. This meant that there was only one CH-53C and two HH-53Cs available to evacuate the marine force on the western beach. This final stage of the operation was noteworthy for the great courage of everyone involved, the fire discipline of the marines on the beach, and the technical skill of the pilots flying the helicopters and supporting warplanes. Sustained fire from the tactical warplanes was controlled by the two forward air-control aircraft, and its accuracy made the Khmer Rouge "keep their heads down." This allowed one CH-53C and one HH-53C to land and collect the first of the departing marines. The HH-53C took off with more than double its standard combat load, and the two helicopters headed at maximum speed for the *Coral Sea*. The other HH-53C arrived and lifted off only a partial load, but saved time by unloading these men on the nearby *Harold E. Holt* after making a very tricky night landing on the destroyer escort's small helicopter platform. The helicopter then returned to the island for another 44 marines, and the last 29 men were lifted out by the CH-53C, which had returned from the *Coral Sea* as rapidly as possible.

Wearing masks in case they had to use CS gas, U.S. Marines board the *Mayaguez* in the hastily planned and executed operation to regain possession of the ship and secure the freedom of her crew.

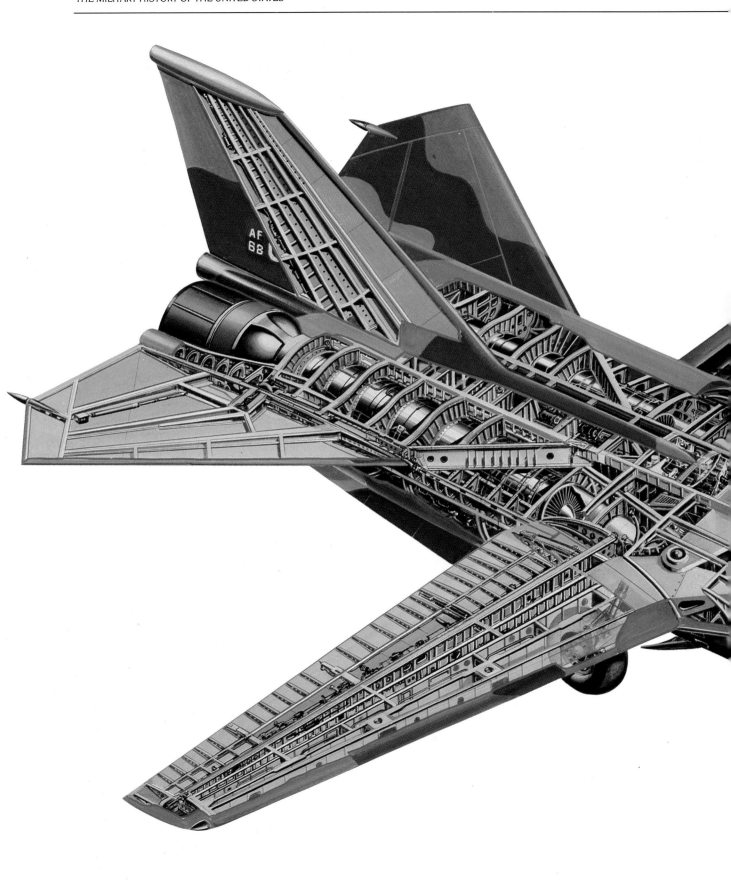

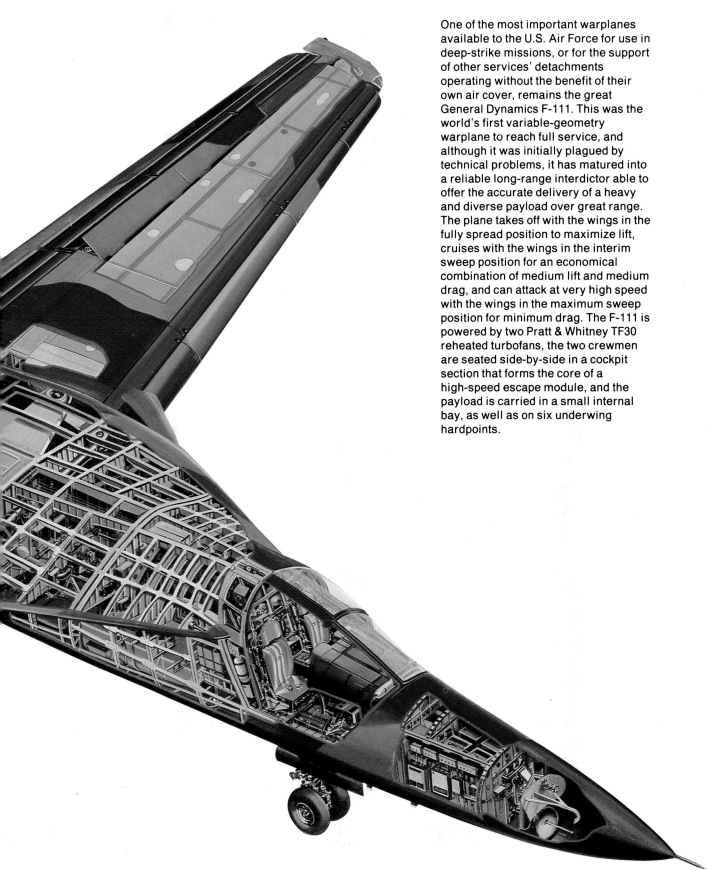

One of the most important warplanes available to the U.S. Air Force for use in deep-strike missions, or for the support of other services' detachments operating without the benefit of their own air cover, remains the great General Dynamics F-111. This was the world's first variable-geometry warplane to reach full service, and although it was initially plagued by technical problems, it has matured into a reliable long-range interdictor able to offer the accurate delivery of a heavy and diverse payload over great range. The plane takes off with the wings in the fully spread position to maximize lift, cruises with the wings in the interim sweep position for an economical combination of medium lift and medium drag, and can attack at very high speed with the wings in the maximum sweep position for minimum drag. The F-111 is powered by two Pratt & Whitney TF30 reheated turbofans, the two crewmen are seated side-by-side in a cockpit section that forms the core of a high-speed escape module, and the payload is carried in a small internal bay, as well as on six underwing hardpoints.

The Tehran Rescue Mission
(1980)

In January 1979, the United States lost one of its major allies in the Middle and Near East when Shah Reza Pahlavi left Iran at the end of an Islamic revolution that saw the accession to power of a Moslem fundamentalist movement headed by the Ayatollah Khomeini. During and after this time, a wave of virulent anti-Americanism swept the country as the Iranian people vented their anger at the nation which had been the main prop of the previous regime. It soon became clear that the Iranians despised the United States, yet it seemed to come as a complete surprise to the American government when Iran broke with the norms of international behavior on November 4, 1979. Angered by the diplomatic asylum granted to the terminally ill ex-Shah by the United States, militant Moslem students seized the American embassy and foreign affairs building in Tehran, the Iranian capital, and in the process took hostage some 66 Americans.

Within five days, President James E. Carter had given permission for the creation of a special joint task force to explore the possibilities for a "military option," a rescue of the hostages by U.S. forces. This was kept completely secret, and the administration started an intense diplomatic effort to secure the release of the hostages. It soon became clear that meaningful negotiation was impossible. An arranged solution to the problem was highly improbable, for the Iranians were concerned solely with their own set of values to the exclusion of accepted international standards. Moreover, the apparent impotence of the United States to dictate a solution was received with delight in Iran and formed the basis of much of that country's massive international propaganda effort.

On January 8, 1980, President Carter told Congress that any "military action that might be orientated toward the release of the hostages would almost certainly end in failure and the death of the hostages." Expressed in a high-profile manner to an august body, this apparent decision against the use of military strength was apparently taken at face value by the Iranians, and certainly by the vast majority of the American people. At the tactical level, it was most useful in maintaining secrecy, for Operation "Ricebowl" had virtually completed the planning phase of the possible rescue attempt. This allowed the first physical preparations for Operation "Eagle Claw," as the rescue attempt was designated, to be made.

Even so, the diplomatic effort was maintained up to April 11, when it was finally conceded that the Iranians were not going to yield to diplomatic pressure.

Enter the Delta Force

With the decision then effectively taken for the "military option" to be exercised at the appropriate time, it was agreed that the appropriate organization to undertake the task was the Delta Force, based at Fort Bragg, North Carolina. This highly secret organization had been created after the end of the Vietnam War, in which the army's Special Forces had in general performed adequately but not outstandingly, and had also revealed a number of important tactical limitations. Inspired by a British unit, the Special Air Service Regiment, the Delta Force was conceived by Colonel Charles A. Beckwith, an American officer who had considerable "elite forces" experience against the communists with the SAS Regiment in the Malayan Emergency of the 1950s, and with the Rangers and Special Forces in the Vietnam War. Beckwith's concept for the Delta Force centered on the increasing need of the United States to counter terrorist organizations and operations, and envisaged the imaginative but low-profile use of small numbers of high-grade troops. Units of this nature were already well established in France, Israel, and West Germany, as well as in the United Kingdom.

Development of the Delta Force proceeded quite rapidly, and most of its individual members had considerable

Jimmy Carter

For further references see pages 75, 80, 81, *82*, 112, 124

Navy personnel of the U.S.S. *Nimitz* complete last-minute checks on one of the Sikorsky RH-53 Sea Stallion helicopters before the launch of the Tehran rescue mission on April 24, 1980.

combat experience. However, in 1980 the unit itself was still young, and was therefore fairly immature and lacking in operational experience.

It was appreciated from the start that "Eagle Claw" was full of difficulties and dangers. Very few senior officers knew about the Delta Force or its operational philosophy, so it was difficult to secure the right kind of cooperation from the services. Much time was also wasted by the political need to examine large numbers of ambitious operational scenarios and reject them tactfully yet firmly as impractical. Another problem that bedeviled the planning was the general belief among those involved that President Carter was not the type of leader to allow the "military option" to be exercised. So the planning proceeded in an aura of unreality and was for this reason somewhat half-hearted as the planners came to believe that things they would like to have happen were probabilities rather than possibilities. The result of this perhaps subconscious feeling was the adoption of "best-case scenarios," instead of the "worst-case scenarios"

generally considered by military planners to be more realistic.

Direct Link to the Joint Chiefs of Staff

So that it could cut through the many bureaucratic levels that would otherwise slow the development of the operation, the Delta Force was subordinated directly to the Joint Chiefs of Staff. This was an eminently sensible decision, but was effectively negated by splitting control of the operation between several commanders with vested interests, and then by failing to appoint a commander with overall authority for the operation in all its aspects.

Another hindrance was the lack of accurate intelligence. At the time of the Shah's overthrow and the general American evacuation from Iran, the Central Intelligence Agency had omitted to leave any stay-behind parties or even agents, so the Delta Force planners were forced to work without precise information about the number of hostages, the

Operation "Eagle Claw:" the bungled-rescue mission into Iran.

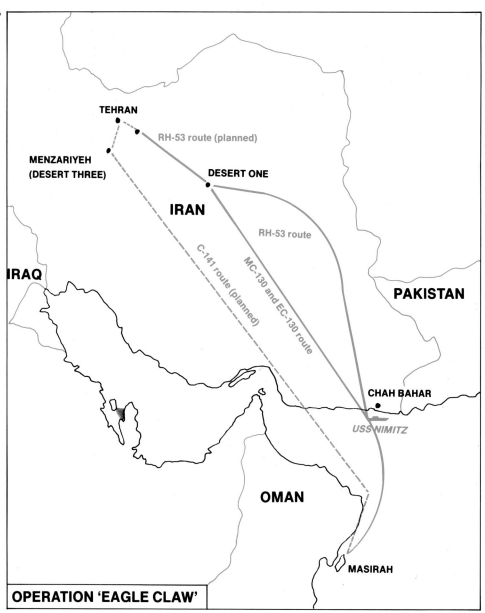

TEHRAN

RH-53 route (planned)

MENZARIYEH
(DESERT THREE)

DESERT ONE

IRAN

RH-53 route

C-141 route (planned)

MC-130 and EC-130 route

IRAQ

PAKISTAN

CHAH BAHAR

USS NIMITZ

OMAN

MASIRAH

OPERATION 'EAGLE CLAW'

areas of the embassy compound in which they were being held, the numbers and locations of their guards, and even the current nature of the embassy and its surroundings. This gave the Delta Force planners the options of infiltrating their own agents into Iran, or of planning the operation with limited – and probably inaccurate – intelligence about an avowedly hostile country.

The planners had a number of operational options open to them, including infiltration from Turkey or a nocturnal parachute drop. The former was rejected because it was politically undesirable to operate from a Turkish base, and the latter because of the inevitably high number of broken limbs that would result from a night drop. The planners examined various other possibilities, but finally opted for a plan based on the use of helicopters.

A Number of Helicopter Options

Here the choice of specific helicopter was difficult, for the planners had to choose between two twin-rotor types (the Boeing Vertol CH-46 Sea Knight and the larger CH-47 Chinook from the same company) and two variants of the single-rotor

The U.S.S. *Nimitz* is the name ship of a planned seven-strong class of aircraft carriers that are the world's largest warships. The *Nimitz* was used to launch the Tehran rescue attempt, and the embarkation of the rescue force's helicopters did not reduce the strength of the carrier's multirole aircraft complement.

Sikorsky H-53 (the HH-53 Super Jolly combat search-and-rescue helicopter and the RH-53D Sea Stallion mine-sweeping helicopter). The planners eventually decided in favor of the RH-53D because of its useful range and great payload: with full fuel, it could carry 30 people, or with reduced fuel, 50 personnel. Stripped of its minesweeping gear, fitted with additional fuel tanks, and equipped with long-range navigation equipment, the RH-53D offered the optimum balance of capabilities. Additional points in favor of the RH-53D were that it was a naval helicopter and would thus not look incongruous on the naval vessels from which the operation would have to be launched, and that it could be maintained without undue difficulty on these naval vessels.

Not surprisingly, the naval pilots of Helicopter Mine Countermeasures Squadron 16 were found to lack the skills needed for high-speed, low-level flight at night over rough terrain and were therefore replaced by pilots of the U.S. Marine Corps' Marine Air Groups 16 and 26 under the command of Colonel Charles H. Pitman. There was some suspicion at first that this was a politically motivated alteration to give the marines some participation in the operation, but flight training over the deserts of Arizona and Nevada soon confirmed that the marines, with Lieutenant Colonel Edward R. Seiffert as lead pilot, were well suited to the task.

Even with additional fuel tanks, the RH-53Ds lacked the range to fly directly from Oman or from an aircraft carrier in nearby waters to the secret staging point in the desert planned for the short flight to Tehran. The first plan to overcome this problem was for the helicopters, loaded with Delta Force troopers, to fly to an intermediate desert spot where they would refuel from bladders dropped by Lockheed C-130 Hercules transport

Final checks are made to a Sikorsky RH-53 Sea Stallion helicopter in the U.S.S. *Nimitz*'s hangar. Even so, helicopter breakdowns jeopardized the mission as the rescue force did not have enough machines to replace damaged ones.

aircraft. Trials in the United States indicated that the bladders often burst when they hit the ground, so an alternative plan had to be devised.

Revised, but Definitive Plans

The planners now decided that the Delta Force troops would fly to the intermediate base in MC-130E "Combat Talon" special forces transports and link up with the helicopters there. The "copters" would fly from their launch carrier before refueling from three EC-130Es, each carrying two 3,000-gallon fuel bladders. The MC-130Es were provided by the 1st, 7th, and 8th Special Operations Squadrons based respectively in the Philippines, West Germany, and Florida, while the EC-130Es were supplied by the 7th Airborne Command & Control Squadron.

As the equipment was organized and the men were gathered and trained, the intelligence picture of the situation in Iran slowly improved. The Iranians released 13 hostages in November 1979, and their

debriefing yielded much useful information that was confirmed and amplified by covert agents introduced under the command of an army officer, Major Richard J. Meadows. Offers of help in the pre-raid intelligence endeavor were received from Delta Force's British and West German counterparts, the SAS Regiment and GSG-9, but rejected. It would be a wholly American operation.

More comprehensive, up-to-date intelligence allowed the planners to finalize details of the operation. The "Desert One" intermediate base, a point in the Iranian desert 305 miles southeast of Tehran, was secretly surveyed by the crew of a STOL transport on March 31 before the final decision was made. This was to be the rendezvous where the RH-53Ds would refuel from the EC-130Es and take on board the Delta Force troopers, who would be delivered by the MC-130Es from Masirah Island off the coast of Oman. The RH-53Ds would then fly to "Desert Two," a point 50 miles southeast of Tehran, arriving shortly before dawn. The Delta Force troopers would be unloaded, and the helicopters would depart to a hiding place with better cover than "Desert Two." The Delta Force troopers would then hide during the day before moving into Tehran by truck during the evening.

The hostages would be freed by a direct assault on the embassy compound and moved by truck to a nearby soccer stadium, where they would be collected by the RH-53Ds. Protection for this stage of the operation would be provided by two AC-130E Hercules gunships: one would circle the embassy compound to deal with any Iranian armored vehicles that tried to intervene and then to destroy the compound after the removal of the hostages; the other would orbit Mehrabad International Airport to prevent the takeoff of the two McDonnell Douglas F-4 Phantom II fighters that the Iranian Air Force had stationed there. At the soccer stadium, the hostages and their Delta Force rescuers would board the RH-53Ds and fly to "Desert Three" southwest of Tehran, the disused airfield at Manzariyeh about halfway between the Iranian capital and the holy city of Qom.

At one stage it had been planned to fly the hostages and Delta Force troopers

Sikorsky RH-53 Sea Stallion helicopters on the flight deck of the U.S.S. *Nimitz* on April 24, 1980.

out of the stadium in a C-130 Hercules transport fitted with rocket-assisted takeoff gear, but the plan was abandoned after the trial airplane crashed. If there were not enough helicopters to ferry all the hostages and rescuers in one lift, the plan was to take the hostages out in one lift and then return for the rescuers, who were also prepared to melt into the background and filter their way out of Iran if possible.

Subsidiary Operation

In preparation for the arrival of the helicopters with the rescued hostages and the Delta Force troopers, "Desert Three" was to be secured by 83 men of Company "C," 1st Battalion, 75th Airborne Ranger Regiment. They would fly in from Masirah Island in three Lockheed C-141A StarLifters that would also carry Major General James B. Vaught, the army officer in command of the operation's Joint Task Force 1-79 structure. The StarLifters were to carry out all the Americans

after the raid. As a back-up to this Ranger detachment, a party of 90 marines, Major Oliver North's Python Force, waited in the eastern Turkish highlands with its helicopters, ready to dash to Tehran or "Desert Three" should the circumstances demand a reinforcement or an alternative plan to extract the hostages and Delta Force troopers.

The entire operation would be completed by just these limited forces if possible. If the rescue turned sour and additional firepower was needed, the U.S. Navy was standing by with Task Force 70, including the nuclear-powered aircraft carrier U.S.S. *Nimitz* with Carrier Air Wing 8 and the conventionally powered aircraft carrier U.S.S. *Coral Sea* with Carrier Air Wing 14. The two air wings had large numbers of Grumman F-14 Tomcat fighters, as well as Grumman A-6 Intruder and Vought A-7 attack warplanes and a small, but technically important, complement of Grumman EA-6B Prowler electronic warfare aircraft. Standing by to treat urgent medical cases would be a McDonnell Douglas C-

The rescue mission gets underway as a Sikorsky RH-53 Sea Stallion helicopter rises from the flight deck of the U.S.S. *Nimitz* with similar machines waiting to follow it.

9A Nightingale aeromedical transport.

The propositioning of some equipment and the major elements of the task force began late in 1979. Six RH-53Ds were airlifted to Diego Garcia, a British island in the Indian Ocean that was one of the forward materiel bases for Central Command. The helicopters were reassembled and thoroughly tested before being embarked on the conventionally powered aircraft carrier U.S.S. *Kitty Hawk*, which was about to take up station in the Arabian Sea. In January 1980, these six copters were transferred to the *Nimitz*, freshly arrived from the United States with another two RH-53Ds.

"Eagle Claw" is Authorized

President Carter authorized the start of "Eagle Claw" on April 16, 1980. Four days later, the Delta Force detachment was flown from Pope Air Force Base, North Carolina, to Rhein-Main Air Base near Frankfurt-am-Main in West Germany. Here the main force was joined by the separate 13-man Special Assault Team of the 10th Special Forces Group. Their

task was to rescue the small number of hostages held in the Foreign Affairs Building in the Tehran embassy compound. On April 21, the complete detachment flew to Wadi Kena in Egypt, from where the complete operation could be controlled via satellite equipment that allowed real-time communication with Washington.

The active part of the operation was to be launched from the *Nimitz* and Masirah Island off the coast of Oman. The RH-53D helicopters were painted in sand camouflage, and the warplanes that might be called in from the *Nimitz* and *Coral Sea* to provide support were given distinctive red flashes on their wings to distinguish them from the same types of aircraft flown by the Iranian Air Force.

The Rescue Attempt Starts

On April 24, 132 men boarded the MC-130Es, commanded by Colonel James H. Kyle, at Masirah airfield. Led by Colonel Beckwith, the emplaned troops included the 93 men of the 1st Special Forces Operations Detachment - Delta, the 13-man Special Assault Team, 12 drivers, 12 men of a road-watch team, and two ex-Imperial Iranian army officers to serve as translators and guides. The first of the MC-130Es took off an hour ahead of the others and crossed the Iranian coast at 400 feet near Chah Bahar. They flew over Iran at low altitude, which the pilots found difficult despite the use of terrain-following radar, inertial navigation systems and forward-looking infrared equipment. Arriving over "Desert One," the crew activated the beacon left by the survey party, landed, and deployed the road-watch team. The plane was scheduled to leave immediately, but it was delayed by the unforeseen arrival of an Iranian civilian bus, which was halted and its 44 occupants detained. Then a fuel truck, possibly involved in a smuggling operation arrived. When its driver refused to stop, the truck was hit with an M72 Light Antitank Weapon, but the driver escaped in a car that had been traveling with the truck. The initial MC-130E then took off and returned to Masirah. There were no further events on the ground at "Desert One" before the next five Hercules transports arrived.

Helicopter Delays and Losses

The eight RH-53Ds should have reached "Desert One" within 30 minutes of the last Hercules. In fact, the helicopters arrived between 60 and 90 minutes later, and not in a single formation but individually and from all directions. Only six helicopters arrived; one had force-landed in the desert with a rotor problem, and another had turned back with flight-control and instrument problems after flying through a severe sandstorm. The remaining six had flown through thick dust clouds, and two had landed and waited for 30 minutes before resuming their flights. Thus the crews of the helicopters were physically and mentally exhausted when they arrived at "Desert One."

Even so, refueling started with a view to continuing the mission as rapidly as possible. A minimum of six helicopters was needed for the mission to go ahead; at this stage a potentially disastrous hydraulic problem was found in one of the six remaining RH-53Ds. Heated discussions followed before President Carter decided that the mission should be aborted and ordered the *Nimitz* to "take any military action necessary to extricate our forces."

Last-minute Catastrophe

The original plan had called for the RH-53Ds to be abandoned at "Desert Three," but it was now decided not to

Iranian military personnel examine the burnt-out wreck of a Sikorsky RH-53 Sea Stallion helicopter in the aftermath of the rescue attempt's failure.

President James E. Carter welcomes the American hostages at an American air base in West Germany after political pressure had finally secured their release. The whole episode effectively destroyed Carter's hopes for a second term as president.

Ronald Reagan

For further references see pages 84, 88, 89, 103, 105, 112, 128

leave the helicopters at "Desert One." The Hercules aircraft had been sitting on the ground with their engines running for more than three hours, and were beginning to run short of fuel. The first of the RH-53Ds to arrive at "Desert One" needed fuel. It lifted off to approach an EC-130, in the process raising a large dust cloud. As it passed over the EC-130E, the helicopter banked, and its main rotor blades sliced into the fuselage of the tanker, causing a huge explosion and a fire that engulfed both machines.

Recovery of the bodies of the eight dead (three in the RH-53D and five in the EC-130) proved impossible because of the fire and exploding ammunition, which combined with flying fragments to damage several other helicopters. The Hercules transports were now too short of fuel to wait any longer for takeoff, so

it was decided to abandon the RH-53Ds as there was not even enough time to destroy them. All the American personnel boarded the surviving Hercules transports and flew back to Masirah Island. Here the casualties were transferred to a C-9A bound for Ramstein Air Base in West Germany, and the other survivors flew to the same base in C-141s. Local commanders asked for an air attack to destroy the RH-53Ds to prevent them from falling into Iranian hands, but the request was vetoed by Washington for fear of injuring the bus passengers who had been detained.

The hostages were finally released by Iran after intense pressure by president-elect Ronald Reagan, and they were finally returned to the United States on January 25, 1981, after a total of 44 days in captivity.

Lt. Gen. James B. Vaught, U.S. Army retired, looks back at the failed hostage rescue mission and addresses the question of why the all-important helicopters broke down.

Gen. Vaught: *That would be a good question for somebody to ask. That question never got asked, and it's one of the ones I certainly wanted to know an answer to. There wasn't any doubt that the commander on that carrier knew he was responsible for those aircraft. You can't tell me that somebody's going to let eight big helicopters wander around on his aircraft carrier and not find out what they're there for and not assume some responsibility for them. I can't believe anybody in the Navy is all that naive, and they aren't. They just didn't do the job. There is just no explicable reason – mechanically or otherwise – why it wasn't just one or two, as some would contend, it was five of the eight helicopters that were not operational or in less than green condition when we got to Desert One (green means ready to fly). One went down on the way. One turned back to the carrier. One went down at Desert One with an oil pump that was not functioning so he couldn't operate the hydraulic system. That's three, and two more in condition amber for one reason or another. We had three helicopters out of eight that were launched in less than five hours of flying time that were fit to fly. That's unheard of. It's absolutely ridiculous, and it wasn't the exigencies of the dust or anything like that. Yes, that slowed them down, but six helicopters got to Desert One and six was all we needed to continue, but we didn't have six operating and we had one that was obviously in condition red and two that were marginal.*

Interviewer: *Did you build a rehearsal site, simulating the embassy compound for the Delta Force to rehearse on?*

Gen. Vaught: *Yes, we did. It wasn't exactly like the embassy compound, but it was about the size and about that complexity, and it was sufficient and we practiced blowing a hole in a wall similar to the one there. We had walls about the same height that they had to scale with ladders in the dark and go the same distances in a kind of environment that would have been very similar to what they would have encountered in Tehran, minus, of course, the thousands of Iranians that would have been around. We couldn't very well go into some big American city somewhere and conduct this. You just couldn't do it and so we did it in an area that was secure, and the only thing*

missing was an opposition force.

Interviewer: *How did you protect this from things like Soviet satellite coverage?*

Gen. Vaught: *We knew their schedule, and when they were up looking, we weren't there. Of course, we didn't do anything in the daytime. We slept most of the time. About 95 percent of everything we did was at night. Anytime we flew in the daytime, it was the regular going from Yuma back to Fort Bragg or something, which is routine flying. As far as practicing components of the mission, we never did that in the daylight. We did it at night. I don't think they had any capabilities to find out what we were doing at night.*

Interviewer: *This structure wasn't something that you built out in the desert that had to be collapsed or anything else was it?*

Gen. Vaught: *Oh yes, we paid attention to that. It wasn't sufficiently similar that they would have noticed it. The things that we added to give it the uniqueness of the compound in Tehran we took down. We didn't leave that up during the day. They couldn't have made the connection, I don't think. I don't believe they did. We had a good OPSEC (operations security). The Iranians and nobody else knew we were there until we told them, and they didn't want to believe it then.*

Vaught also addressed the question of competency.

I had competent people in charge who trained for what it was they were going to do; who knew what we had to do; and who were motivated to do it. If it started to come apart, they knew what to do. To wit: after the decision was made that we could not go on and we had to come out of Desert One and everybody was notified, and they started to reposition the helicopter and it was crashed into the 130, and we had a big fire and the Delta guys got off and scattered around the desert, and reloaded on the aircraft. We got every living, swinging being, and we logged this in, every American was out of that desert in 22 minutes. We pulled in the security and released the hostages and did all these things and still got out of there. Now, if that's a disorganized unit that doesn't know who its leaders are and is totally confused when challenged, then we need a lot more of them. I'd say that it was an organization that knew what it was doing and how to do it and had superb people leading it and reacted to unforeseen contingencies that stretched the imagination. We got it done.

The Invasion of Grenada
(1983)

Maurice Bishop

For further references
see pages
86, 89, 90

A Sikorsky CH-53 Sea Stallion assault transport helicopter of the U.S. Marines Corps is readied for takeoff from the amphibious assault ship U.S.S. *Guam* during Operation "Urgent Fury."

When the tiny island of Grenada in the Windward Islands in the southeastern Caribbean was granted independence by the British in 1974, it was dominated by the personality of Sir Eric Gairy, a former trade unionist who became prime minister of a government notable for a very eccentric foreign policy and a domestic policy of political repression and great corruption. In March 1979, this regime was toppled by the well-respected Maurice Bishop in a bloodless coup by the Provisional Revolutionary Government based on Bishop's New JEWEL (Joint Endeavour for Welfare, Education and Liberation) Movement Party.

Like most new leaders, Bishop faced a host of political and economic problems.

The New JEWEL Movement government took the communist regime of Cuba as its model, and over the next four years, it invited and received considerable aid, both financial and material, from Cuba as well as a number of other communist countries. This aroused deep suspicion for the Grenadian government from the U.S. administration, and this suspicion was deepened in the mind of President Ronald Reagan's advisors by the Grenadian government's steadfast refusal to hold democratic elections. These affronts to U.S. foreign policy in the region were made worse when the Grenadian government announced its intention to create a new international airport at Point Salines in the extreme south of the island.

Key Factor: The New Airport

The airport was to be built by a Cuban work force, but its most worrying feature was the planned 9,800-foot--long runway. It would be long enough to

A trooper of the 82nd Airborne Division applies camouflage to his face and neck as his unit relaxes on a ridge behind the new airfield at Point Salines.

handle the largest aircraft in the world, far beyond the requirements of the tourist trade that brought most aircraft to Grenada. The American government suspected – rightly – that Cuban involvement meant that the new airport would also serve a military purpose as a staging point for Cuban aircraft ferrying troops, specialists, and equipment to the revolutionary forces in Africa, and for Soviet aircraft bound for the new communist enclave in Nicaragua. Work on the airport started in 1979 and was scheduled to end in 1984.

By 1983, however, the New JEWEL Movement government was facing acute problems as a result of its connection with the communist bloc. The military and paramilitary forces had certainly benefitted from the connection; by this time, the Grenadian People's Revolutionary Armed Forces were larger and better equipped that the combined forces of all Grenada's neighbors in the eastern Caribbean, and there were plans to

expand these forces still more. On the other hand, the support of Cuba and eastern European communist states had done nothing for the ordinary Grenadian; it had been devoted to developing Grenada's usefulness as a political and logistic base in the region. Moreover, the arrogant behavior of the numerous Cuban advisers on the island was steadily alienating the Grenadian civilian population.

The dispute about continued affiliation with the communist bloc had split the New JEWEL Movement by the third quarter of 1983. Bishop was the leader of the section of the party now unhappy with Grenada's communist links, and he urged that closer links should be forged with the western bloc. Bernard Coard, the deputy prime minister, led the faction which was convinced that communism was the answer to Grenada's problems, and that the country should be converted as rapidly as possible into a Marxist state.

The dispute reached a head on

A marine mans his 7·62-mm (0·3-inch) caliber Browning machine gun in the doorway of a Boeing Vertol CH-46 Sea Knight helicopter, ready to provide suppressive fire should his helicopter come under antiaircraft fire while attempting to land.

October 13. Coard had already won the support of General Hudson Austin, commander of the Grenadian forces, and ordered Bishop to resign. Bishop, charged with failure to implement the commands of the New JEWEL Movement's Central Committee, was immediately placed under house arrest. Several ministers who supported Bishop resigned; they, too, were arrested.

The Grenadian Regime Falls Out of Favor

News of these events angered many Grenadian citizens, and over the following days, there were large pro-Bishop demonstrations in several parts of the island. There were indications that the militia was restless, and a general strike was called for the work force in St. George's, the capital. Matters continued to deteriorate, and on October 18, most of the island's students were involved in a large anti-Coard demonstration in St. George's. As the unrest continued, Unison Whiteman, the foreign minister, broke off a trip to New York, where he was scheduled to address the United Nations Organization, and added his voice to those calling for Bishop's release. On October 19, Whiteman spoke to a gathering in the streets of St. George's, and as news of the event spread, more Grenadians arrived. The large crowd

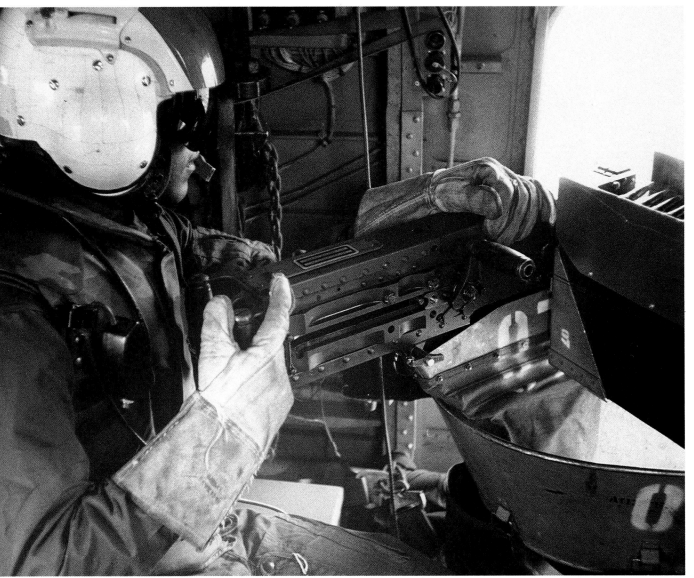

decided to free Bishop from house arrest in his official residence at Mount Royal. The ex-prime minister's guards initially resisted the pressure of the crowd and fired over their heads in a vain effort to halt them. But realizing that numbers were against them, the guards then permitted the crowd to free Bishop.

Whiteman persuaded Bishop to return with the crowd to St. George's, where several other ex-ministers were thought to be imprisoned in Fort Ruppert, originally part of the harbor defenses and now a main base for the People's Revolutionary Army. Already informed of Bishop's release, the guards at Fort Ruppert decided to offer no resistance, laid down their weapons, and allowed the crowd to enter the fortress and release the ex-ministers.

Unnecessary Massacre

The situation now became more threatening. Three Soviet-built armored personnel carriers and a truckload of People's Revolutionary Army soldiers arrived in front of the fort. Officer Cadet Conrad Meyers deployed his men in front of the fort and ordered them to fire on the crowd. More than 100 civilians were killed as the soldiers opened fire and in the panic-struck flight that followed. There were also casualties among the soldiers, of whom three were killed including Meyers. As the crowd fled, the soldiers moved in to rearrest the freed leaders. Bishop and four of the ex-ministers, and three of their leading supporters, were led into the fort and killed. Jacqueline Creft, the ex-minister of education, was beaten to death; the others were shot as they knelt on the edge of a basketball court. The authorities now imposed a 24-hour curfew and warned that anyone violating it would be shot without warning.

During the evening, General Austin made a radio broadcast announcing the creation of a Revolutionary Military Council headed by himself. Althiugh it was rumored that Coard had fled, he was in fact Austin's adviser at this time. The curfew was extended to four days while the agents of the Revolutionary Military Council rounded up everyone thought to

be a threat, real or imagined, to the new regime. The bodies of Bishop and the other seven people killed at Fort Ruppert were taken to the east coast of the island and secretly buried in the garbage dump at Calivigny Camp.

News of events in Grenada spread rapidly to other islands of the region, causing a spreading wave of revulsion toward the island's new regime. Newspapers demanded a boycott and embargo of Grenada, and regional leaders met to discuss a response to the events. On October 21, the government heads of the six states forming the Organization of Eastern Caribbean States came together in Bridgetown, Barbados, under the chairmanship of Eugenia Charles, the president of Dominica. The organization decided on the short-term expedient of sanctions against Grenada, but also concluded that military intervention was necessary. Since its member nations (Antigua, Dominica, Montserrat, St. Kitts-Nevis, St. Lucia, and St. Vincent) lacked the necessary forces, the organization therefore appealed to Barbados, Jamaica, and the United States for assistance, as allowed in the organization's charter.

On October 22, a meeting of the Caribbean Community States was held in Port of Spain, Trinidad. Its delegates voted to ask Grenada for permission to send a fact-finding mission and a Caribbean peacekeeping force, or failing that, a full military intervention.

Since the beginning of the unrest that had led to the fall of Bishop, the United States had been maintaining a careful watch over Grenadian affairs. In addition to strategic concern for the region, there were fears for some 1,000 American citizens on the island. Most were faculty members or students at St. George's University Medical School, an institution providing training for medical students unable to attend American medical schools. On October 19, the Joint Chiefs of Staff warned Admiral W. McDonald, the commander-in-chief of the Atlantic Fleet, to prepare a plan for the evacuation of noncombatants and to consider possible courses of action. The following day, the Special Situations Group of the National Security Council met to decide on the recommendations it should make to President Reagan. As contingency planning continued, a note of urgency was injected. The request of the Organization of Eastern Caribbean States for assistance was received, which made a military response probable rather than possible.

Rapid Response is Essential

The rapid development of the Grenadian crisis meant that any military operation would have to be mounted with forces readily available in the region. Fortunately, there was more than adequate naval strength; two U.S. Navy task forces were in the area on their way to the Mediterranean. The first was Captain Carl R. Erie's Task Force 124, centered on the amphibious helicopter carrier U.S.S. *Guam* and four landing ships carrying the 1,700 marines of Colonel James P. Faulkner's 22nd Marine Amphibious Unit. They were scheduled to relieve the 24th Marine Amphibious Unit currently

deployed at Beirut International Airport as part of the Multinational Peacekeeping Force in Lebanon. The 22nd Marine Amphibious Unit was fully prepared for action with vital equipment such as landing craft, tanks, and amphibious tractors. The key components of the unit were Lieutenant Colonel Ray L. Smith's Battalion Landing Team 2/8 (the 2nd Battalion of the 8th Marine Regiment) together with one battery of artillery, and the helicopters of the reinforced HMM-261 squadron.

The second of the naval groupings available in the region was Rear Admiral Richard C. Berry's carrier battle group centered on the U.S.S. *Independence* (with Carrier Air Wing 6) and including escorting cruisers and destroyers. Both task forces had sailed on October 18, and on October 21 were ordered closer to Grenada.

The original plan was a routine evacuation of American nationals by these forces alone. Such an operation called for the marines to provide local security as U.S. civilians were collected

Men of the 82nd Airborne Division are airlifted into their landing zone by helicopter during Operation ''Urgent Fury.''

Joseph Metcalf III

For further references
see pages
90, *94*, 96

Marines aboard an
LVTP7 (Landing
Vehicle Tracked
Personnel Mk 7) near
the town of St.
George's on October
28, 1983, during
Operation ''Urgent
Fury.''

and transported to Pearls Airport on
the north of the island, where they
would be lifted by helicopter to the
Guam and then transported to Barbados.
The plan was sound enough in principle, but it depended on the agreement of the Grenadian authorities. Such
agreement now seemed increasingly unlikely. The 22nd Marine Amphibious Unit
thus seemed too small for the task,
given the possible opposition of the
Grenadian forces. These included the
People's Revolutionary Army, variously
estimated at anything between 1,200 and
1,500 men, and a militia of between 2,000
and 5,000. The U.S. planners also had to
take into account the presence on the
island of some 700 Cubans, whose precise
nature and intentions remained unknown.

Reagan Opts for Intervention

President Reagan decided on October 22
that military intervention was necessary,
and it was only at this stage that warn-

ing orders went out to other elements
of the American military establishment
for the planning and implementation on
October 25 of what became Operation
''Urgent Fury.'' The campaign was the
responsibility of Joint Task Force 120,
commanded by Vice Admiral Joseph Metcalf III with Major General H. Norman
Schwarzkopf as his second-in-command
controlling ground operations. The planners had less than 48 hours to prepare
a complex undertaking that was now to
involve U.S. Army and U.S. Navy special forces under the command of Major
General R.L. Scholtes, the U.S. Army's 82nd
Airborne Division under the command of
Major General Edward L. Trobaugh, and
substantial assets of the U.S. Air Force,
under the command of Brigadier General
R.B. Patterson, for the movement and support of the combined forces.

In Grenada, the Revolutionary Military
Council had met on October 20 to plan its
future course of action. Its two major
tasks were winning over the island's
population and resisting any invasion.

The curfew was lifted temporarily to allow people to shop for food, and on October 22 the radio service broadcast an odd apology for current events, as well as an invented admission by Bishop supporters that they had been responsible for the massacre. The latter was produced from tape recordings that had been so badly doctored that most listeners thought that the speakers were either drugged or being tortured, which added to the mistrust already felt toward the Revolutionary Military Council.

Cuba Sits on the Fence

The council knew that it had little to fear from the Organization of Eastern Caribbean States or the Caribbean Community, but it was rightly concerned about the presence in none-too-distant waters of powerful American forces. These the People's Revolutionary Army could not hope to defeat, so the Revolutionary Military Council waited with great urgency for the reaction of Cuba to the killing of Bishop and other recent events. These incidents presented President Fidel Castro with a difficult problem: while Bishop had been presented to the Cuban people as a hero, it would jeopardize the Cuban investment in Grenada to denounce the regime that had killed him. The Cuban authorities sought to sit on the fence, the massacre and later killings were reported as "atrocious acts." Cuba called for "exemplary punishment" of those responsible, but at the same time did not condemn the Revolutionary Military Council. On October 21, General Austin sent a personal message to Castro, pointing out the danger of an invasion by the U.S.A. and requesting Cuban troops to fight under Grenadian command.

Austin received his reply on October 22 via the Cuban ambassador, who took the Revolutionary Military Council to task for creating this unnecessary crisis. He said that it was impossible to send Cuban troops to the island, certainly not to fight under Grenadian command, but then added that Cuba's reputation as a leader of third-world communism was at stake. In these cir-

cumstances, the Cubans already on the island were at the disposal of the Revolutionary Military Council. Advisers to the People's Revolutionary Army would fight with that force, and the workers at Point Salines would defend that area, but under Cuban rather than People's Revolutionary Armed Forces' command.

Official Request for Aid

At much the same time, another factor entered the equation. Sir Paul Scoon, the island's governor-general, smuggled out a letter requesting external assistance to protect him and his staff and to restore order. Scoon had been largely ignored by the People's Revolutionary Government and the Revolutionary Military Council, and was effectively relegated to Government House. However, as the U.S. government did not recognize the Revolutionary Military Council, it could now accept Scoon's letter as an official request by the island's highest authority.

On October 23, the Cubans were issued with heavy weapons from Grenadian stocks. They blocked the runway at Point Salines with oil drums and other equipment and started preparing defensive positions. The Revolutionary Military Council was worried about the loyalty of the militia and therefore decided to use only the People's Revolutionary Army for its active defense of the island.

On the same day, Metcalf and Schwarzkopf arrived on the *Guam* and briefed its navy and marine staffs on the new plan, which was modeled on an exercise undertaken two years earlier. The plan divided Grenada into two halves, with the navy and marine corps responsible for the northern part and the army and air force for the southern part. The first objective – the security of the Americans on the island – was made more difficult by the fact that the medical school had two separate campuses, with an uncertain number of Americans on each.

At the operation's start on October 25, the marines would make amphibious and helicopter landings to secure Pearls Airport. At the same time, men of

Norman Schwarzkopf

For further references see pages 89, 96

the U.S. Army's 75th Airborne Ranger Infantry Regiment would seize Point Salines Airport: one company would make a parachute landing, and other men would arrive by Lockheed C-130 Hercules transports that would land and, while taxiing, disgorge armed jeeps. With the airport secured, a battalion of the 82nd Airborne Division would arrive by air. Finally, the Caribbean Peacekeeping Force, reinforced by other elements of the 82nd Airborne Division, would arrive from Barbados.

Special Forces Raids

At the same time as the initial landings, the American special forces would undertake three separate but important missions, two of them by the navy's SEAL Team Six and the other by the

army's 1st. Special Operations Detatchment - Delta. As the two Ranger battalions and the relevant elements of the 82nd Airborne Division completed their preparations in the United States, the special forces were prepositioned in Grenada using the HALO (High Altitude Low Opening) parachuting technique. One of the aircraft involved in this operation missed its drop zone, and a number of SEALs landed in the sea. Four of them became tangled in their parachutes and drowned. Raids One and Two were entrusted to the SEALs: the rescue of Scoon and his movement to a point of safety (the house of a retired British officer on the island), and the destruction of Radio Free Grenada's transmitter. Raid Three, allocated to the troopers of the Delta Force supported by the helicopters of the 101st Airborne Division's 160th

Men of the 82nd Airborne Division board a Lockheed C-141 Starlifter transport at Point Salines on November 4, 1963.

A Sikorsky CH-53 Sea Stallion helicopter hovers beside the Soviet-supplied antiaircraft equipment it has come to collect. The ZU-23 is a light, manually operated piece of equipment carrying two 23-mm cannon which can be highly effective against targets such as helicopters.

Aviation Battalion, involved an attack on Richmond Hill Prison, which was virtually surrrounded by People's Revolutionary Army installations such as Fort Frederick, the army headquarters. The helicopters were to neutralize the guards and so permit the troopers to make a ground assault that would secure the prisoners and prepare them for evacuation.

A group of American and British consular officials had earlier arrived to evaluate the situation and arrange for an evacuation of civilians. This party left Pearls Airport on October 24, just before the arrival of a Soviet-built transport carrying Colonel Pedro Tortola Comas. He was to assume command of the Cuban forces on Grenada, which amounted to 53 military advisers and 636 construction workers. Some 784 other Cubans were under orders to remain indoors, and 50 other Cuban dependants were moved to the *Vietnam Herico*, a Cuban mer-

chant ship lying in St. George's Harbor.

The Revolutionary Military Council tried a last attempt at diplomacy, using an out-of-date telex directory to send two messages not to their intended recipient, the Foreign and Commonwealth Office in London, but to a manufacturer of plastic bags in another part of the British capital.

Tardy Reconnaissance

The assault areas were reconnoitered on the night of October 24-25, and confirmed that an earlier reconnaissance had been right so far as the marine areas were concerned. To avoid alerting the Cubans to the Point Salines landing, though, no earlier reconnaissance had been undertaken, so it was only at this late hour that the blocking of the runway was discovered. This demanded a major alteration of the Ranger and airborne

soldiers' effort, which now had to be undertaken wholly as a paradrop without any C-130 landings.

Heavy Antiaircraft Fire

The landing at Pearls Airport and nearby Grenville went according to plan, and the speed and intensity of the marines' helicopter attack ensured that all objectives were secured with minimal casualties. Greater opposition met the Ranger and airborne force heading for Point Salines Airport, where heavy antiaircraft fire rose to meet the 13 American aircraft (three AC-130 gunships and 13 C-130 transports). Even so, the gunships effectively suppressed the antiaircraft guns, and the U.S. soldiers jumped onto the airport. A last-minute change of plan resulted in a confused drop, but the Americans were aided by the Cubans' poor tactical dispositions. The Cubans had not expected an airborne operation and left only one company to hold the airport while the other two manned the beach defenses. The Americans soon cleared the airport area and fought off a Cuban counterattack. They began clearing the runway as a radio message was sent to Pope Air Force Base, South Carolina, for additional elements of the 82nd Airborne Division to be flown in.

Over the same period, the three special forces raids were launched. None went according to plan. The most successful was Raid Two, in which the SEALs reached the transmitter compound later than scheduled. They closed down the radio service, which was broadcasting orders mobilizing the militia and calling all

Men of the 82nd Airborne Division's organic artillery component fire their 105-mm (4·12-in) M102 howitzers during Operation "Urgent Fury" on November 3, 1983.

medical personnel to duty. Raid Three was carefully coordinated with the Point Salines landing, but the revision of the latter's plan and the consequent delay had allowed the local defenders to be warned. As a result, the helicopter attack designed to suppress the defenses was met by intense fire, which shot down one Sikorsky UH-60 Black Hawk and one Hughes Model 500 helicopter. This raid was therefore called off as the planners feared that further efforts might result in the execution of the prisoners it was designed to rescue.

Raid One scored an initial success as 22 SEALs reached Government House and took both Scoon and his staff under their protection. Then the People's Revolutionary Army commander, who had failed to prevent the SEALs from reaching Government House, called for reinforcements, including three armored personnel carriers, and it became clear that the SEALs and their rescuees were trapped.

Unfortunately, Government House was within range of the antiaircraft guns at Forts Frederick and Ruppert, so gunship support would be difficult and dangerous. It was decided instead to send helicopter gunships that could possibly operate under the fire of the antiaircraft guns. Two Bell AH-1T SeaCobras arrived, but the first was downed. The second called in a medevac helicopter and guided it in as an AC-130 partially suppressed the antiaircraft guns, but was itself then shot down as the medevac helicopter lifted off. The People's Revolutionary Army then attacked Government House, and the SEALs called in an AC-130 that destroyed one of the BTR-60 armored personnel carriers and halted the attack. A stalemate followed.

Admiral Metcalf ordered a heavy attack on the defenses of St. George's by Vought A-7E Corsair IIs from the *Independence*. This action caused considerable damage

Vice Admiral Joseph Metcalf, commanding Task Force 120, talks to a group of U.S. Army Rangers during Operation "Urgent Fury" on October 26, 1983, although the conversation is interrupted by the takeoff of a Lockheed C-141B StarLifter from Point Salines.

Left: A marine armed with an M16A1 assault rifle stands guard over a captured member of the People's Revolutionary Army on Carriacou Island off Grenada on November 2, 1983. Other marines search the trunk of the captured man's automobile for weapons and/or incriminating evidence.

Below: Photographed by a member of the Navy Combat Camera Team, marines search a member of the People's Revolutionary Army after his capture on Carriacou Island on November 28, 1983.

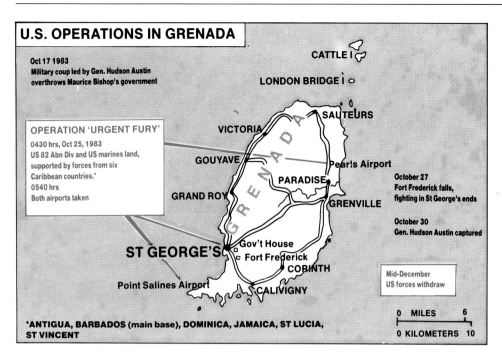

U.S. OPERATIONS IN GRENADA

Oct 17 1983
Military coup led by Gen. Hudson Austin
overthrows Maurice Bishop's government

OPERATION 'URGENT FURY'
0430 hrs, Oct 25, 1983
US 82 Abn Div and US marines land,
supported by forces from six
Caribbean countries.'
0540 hrs
Both airports taken

CATTLE I

LONDON BRIDGE I

SAUTEURS

VICTORIA

GOUYAVE

Pearls Airport

PARADISE

October 27
Fort Frederick falls,
fighting in St George's ends

GRAND ROY

GRENVILLE

October 30
Gen. Hudson Austin captured

ST GEORGE'S — Gov't House
Fort Frederick

CORINTH

Point Salines Airport

CALIVIGNY

Mid-December
US forces withdraw

0 MILES 6
0 KILOMETERS 10

*ANTIGUA, BARBADOS (main base), DOMINICA, JAMAICA, ST LUCIA,
ST VINCENT

Operation ''Urgent
Fury:'' the American
invasion of Grenada.

and knocked out most of the antiaircraft guns, but also hit Fort Matthew. This site was painted identically to nearby Fort Ruppert and flew the flag of the People's Revolutionary Army, but it was in fact a mental hospital. Several of the patients were killed, and others escaped to roam the adjacent area over the next few days.

Grenadian Morale High

The morale of the People's Revolutionary Army was high, for despite the failure to halt the marines at Pearls Airport and Grenville, it had beaten off two other attacks and had the SEAL team trapped in Government House. The Grenadians also wrongly believed that the Cubans had defeated the American landing at Point Salines Airport, where additional men of the 82nd Airborne division in fact began to arrive in the early afternoon. Unloading was difficult because of the limited runway length available and Cuban sniper fire, but gradually American numbers in this airhead increased, and a detachment reached and secured the True Blue campus of the medical school. The staff members were now able to help the medical personnel of the Ranger and the airborne division, and interviews with the students helped to clarify the situation at the Grand Anse campus.

During this period and the following night, the airhead was further expanded and reinforced with elements of the 82nd Airborne Division's 2nd Brigade as well as 105-mm. (4·13-inch) caliber artillery.

The most immediate task facing Metcalf was the rescue of the SEAL team trapped with the governor general and his staff in Government House. At Schwarzkopf's suggestion, the marine company on board the U.S.S. *Manitowoc*, unused in the Pearls Airport landing, extemporized a company-strength landing in Grand Mal Bay, just north of St. George's, early on October 26 to link up with another company that had been ferried across the island by helicopter. The two companies then moved on Government House and relieved those trapped there. The SEALs and the rescuees were then evacuated to the *Guam*, and the marines moved south to take the racetrack at Queen's Park, where a helicopter landing zone was created.

Students are Rescued

It had become clear during the night that there were about 200 students at the Grand Anse campus, and their rescue became Metcalf's second priority of October 26. Radio messages warned the students to ready themselves for evacuation, and in the afternoon a line of helicopters swept into the campus. A Boeing-Vertol CH-46 Sea Knight was knocked down by antiaircraft fire, but the guns were soon silenced by attacks delivered by A-7 Corsair IIs and their heavier-weight counterparts, Grumman A-6E Intruders. After a short firefight, the Rangers smashed their way into the campus and rescued the students. The loss of the helicopter had left the rescuers short of airlift capability, so 12 Rangers stayed behind so that all the students could be helicoptered out. The Rangers avoided capture, seized a fishing boat, and headed out to sea, where they were collected by the destroyer U.S.S. *Caron.*

At Point Salines Airport, most of October 26 was spent in expanding and consolidating the airhead before the 82nd Airborne Division moved out to the north. American radio operators intercepted requests to the Cuban authorities for per-

mission to surrender, but Havana curtly refused, and some brisk firefights followed before many Cubans gave themselves up. The American troops soon found quantities of arms and other equipment far too large for any envisaged use on Grenada, which were clearly destined for the areas of Africa where Cuban forces were fighting.

On October 27, the Americans continued "Urgent Fury" and there was a further advance from Point Salines Airport, where a third airborne battalion landed; marine positions in and around St. George's were developed further, and the marine position near Pearls Airport was improved by the capture of the Mount Horne Agricultural Station, where large quantities of weapons were discovered. A feature of the day's operations was the collapse of morale among the men of the People's Revolutionary Army: many abandoned their weapons and uniforms. They

Sikorsky CH-53 Sea Stallion helicopters of the U.S. Marine Corps arrive to evacuate American medical students from Grenada on October 26, 1983.

American students wait patiently for the aircraft that will take them away from trouble-torn Grenada. In the foreground, a U.S. soldier stands guard with an M60 machine gun.

donned civilian clothes and tried to melt into the civilian population, which saw the Americans as liberators and saw no reason to aid or shelter their own troops that they had come to regard as oppressors. The largest undertaking of the day was an airmobile attack on the Calivigny Barracks by a reinforced element of the 2nd Battalion of the 75th Airborne Ranger Infantry Regiment.

With Calivigny Barracks in American hands and the People's Revolutionary Army finally expelled from St. George's, the southern half of the island was secure and a large part of the northern half under firm marine control. ''Urgent Fury''

ended on October 30 after the U.S. forces had spent three days in a sweep through the rest of the island to mop up the last pockets of resistance.

The first elements of the Caribbean Peacekeeping Force arrived on October 29, and soon the American forces were being pulled out of Grenada in a program completed by mid-December. The operation had cost the lives of 18 American servicemen (11 soldiers, three marines, and four SEALs), and another soldier later died of his wounds. Another 116 men were wounded. The Cubans lost 25 dead and 59 wounded, and Grenadian losses were about 25 dead and 350 wounded.

Private first class, 2nd Battalion, 75th Ranger Infantry Regiment, U.S. Army, Grenada, 1983

Although the origins of the Rangers can be traced back to the French and Indian Wars of the mid-18th century, the modern Ranger concept dates from World War II, when six Ranger battalions were created as commando-type units modeled on the British pattern. These Ranger battalions were disbanded after World War II, but the concept made a small-scale comeback during the Korean War at company level before being disbanded at the end of that war. The title Ranger was then reserved for graduates of the U.S. Army's Ranger School at Fort Benning, Georgia. The school taught fieldcraft and mountaineering under adverse geographic and climatic conditions, and the men who passed the course received a black/yellow shoulder flash for their uniforms. In the Vietnam War, the Long-Range Reconnaissance Units formed by individual commands later became Ranger Companies under the administrative wing of the 75th Ranger Infantry Regiment. In the mid-1970s, two permanent Ranger battalions were formed as the 1st Battalion, 75th Ranger Infantry Regiment at Fort Stewart, Georgia, and the 2nd Battalion, 75th Ranger Infantry Regiment at Fort Lewis, Washington. This soldier wears Vietnam War-era jungle fatigues with jungle boots and the M1951 olive drab patrol cap. The two Ranger battalions are the last U.S. Army units to retain this cap. The other two major items of kit are the ALICE (All-purpose Lightweight Individual Combat Equipment) nylon webbing with belt and suspenders, and the special grenadier vest used only by the 2nd Ranger Battalion. The latter was developed by a private contractor and issued free to the battalion, and it contains numerous pouches for carrying ammunition magazines and grenades. The soldier's weapon is the 5·56-mm (0·22-inch) caliber M16A1 assault rifle with underslung 40-mm M203 grenade launcher, and he also carries M67 grenades on each side of the ammunition pouches.

Secretary of Defense Weinberger held a press conference to explain the Grenada operation:

Secretary Weinberger: *Good afternoon, ladies and gentlemen. I wanted to take your questions this afternoon about the various activities in Grenada. Before doing that I would just say that the operations are progressing extremely well. The army and the marine corps units are moving against the remaining few objectives, against diminishing Cuban resistance. We have not secured all of the objectives but we believe we will before very much longer.*

We have rescued and are transferring back to the United States a number of Americans. The first flight will have about 70 and they will go to Charleston (SC). And we have control now, as you know, of both airfields, and one campus of the Medical College and we were very pleased to be able to release the Governor General and his wife and his family. They are safe and were out on the Guam *a few hours ago.*

And, of course, we've captured about 600 Cubans, many of them combatants, almost all of whom were with rifles who were shooting at us, and a large number of weapons including a number of Soviet AK-47s.

We've also overrun and taken what appears to be a major Cuban installation near a little place called Frequente and at that place a Cuban colonel was taken prisoner. A large amount of command and control equipment, radios, secret documents, and things of that kind were all found there.

The principle areas of resistance still are at Richmond Hill which is the prison here and at this beach area near the second campus of the medical school. Almost all of the American citizens who were evacuated, the 70 group that I mentioned and the others, have been students.

There are approximately 3,000 U.S. and other nation forces on the ground in the area. Casualties thus far have been: killed 6, missing 8, wounded 33. We have been in touch through our interest section in Havana trying to arrange the safe evacuation of the very large number of Cuban prisoners and have not been able to get in touch with them to get that completed yet.

I believe those are the only points I would want to make. General Vessey, do you have anything you wanted to add?

General Vessey: *I was just handed a note, Mr. Secretary, saying that the rescue of the students at the Grand Ance Campus of the Medical College is underway and six helicopter loads of students have been evacuated.*

Secretary Weinberger: *That's the one we were most concerned with, and of course, if that had been a group of empty buildings it would have been taken last night, but we wanted to be as careful as possible, and I'm delighted. That would leave the primary area of resistance then at the Richmond Hill Prison. We'd be glad to take questions.*

Q: *General Vessey, we understand that when you landed, when the Rangers landed on Tuesday morning they encountered not just armed Cuban construction workers but in fact a combat battalion that had dug in very well prepared positions and put up fierce resistance. Did you anticipate meeting organized Cuban military units and what did you do to offset the apparent surprise?*

Gen. Vessey: *No, we didn't anticipate meeting Cuban fighting units. We knew there were Cuban construction workers in there who might have been reservists and might have been armed, but the first planes coming into the area received antiaircraft fire, which is a contrast to the statements coming out of Havana which say that they have only construction workers in Grenada.*

Secretary Weinberger: *Incidentally, as you know I'm sure, Havana radio has been on the air stating that Cuban resistance on the island ended today. Some of the Cubans on the island don't quite seem to have heard the broadcast.*

The Lebanese Intervention (1982-1984)

The U.S. Navy's amphibious transport dock U.S.S. *Nashville* is pictured off the coast of Lebanon during the multinational peacekeeping operation in Beirut. The ship was deployed to the region after the 1982 confrontation between Israeli forces and the "fighters" of the Palestine Liberation Organization.

Starting before "Urgent Fury," but continuing until after it, was another American involvement in the turbulent affairs of Lebanon. Lebanon, a country of 3 million people occupying a beautiful land with a long coastline on the eastern side of the Mediterranean, could have been an oasis of prosperous stability among its troubled neighbors, but its own internal problems were compounded by the spill-over of other struggles on its borders.

Within Lebanon there was a long-standing dispute between the country's Christians and Moslems, but this comparatively simple dichotomy was actually considerably more difficult and dangerous. There were in the country two major Christian factions (the Maronite

Christians of the Beirut area and the Christians of southern Lebanon), two major Islamic factions (the Druze and the Shi'as), and several smaller Islamic factions. Further complication was added by the presence of large numbers of Palestinians, most of them in squatter camps and heavily involved in the Palestine Liberation Organization's war with Israel; a Syrian army of occupation in the Bekaa valley on the eastern side of the country; and a toothless United Nations Interim Force.

The Palestinians had been ejected from Jordan in 1970 by King Hussein after their interference in Jordanian matters. With Syrian assistance they had moved into southern and central Lebanon. The Palestinians had sought to manipulate the various Islamic factions; Israel responded with support for the Christian factions. This led in 1975 to a civil war, and, in 1976, the Syrians, fearing that Israel might take advantage of this fact to invade the country, occupied much of the eastern side of northern and central Lebanon. The internecine fighting be-

Sikorsky CH-53 Sea Stallion helicopters prepare to lift off from the amphibious assault ship U.S.S. *Guam* in November 1983. The ship operated off the Lebanese coast to provide support for U.S. forces involved in the multinational peacekeeping force in Beirut. One of seven ''Iwo Jima'' class LPHs (Landing Platforms, Helicopter) derived ultimately from the escort carrier of World War II, the *Guam* can carry a battalion landing team of 1,746 men (144 officers and 1,602 enlisted men) plus most of its equipment, artillery and vehicles. Ship-to-shore movement capability is provided by 20 Boeing Vertol CH-46 Sea Knight or 11 Sikorsky CH-53 Sea Stallion assault transport helicopters.

tween Lebanon's factions continued, and the Palestinians were able to create a virtual state within a state as a base for their operations against Israel. The United Nations Interim Force in Lebanon tried to police the fluid ''interface'' between Israel and its northern neighbors, but could not prevent the movement of Palestinians into and out of northern Israel.

Israeli Exasperation

The continued Palestinian attacks on targets in Galilee exasperated the Israeli government of Prime Minister Menachem Begin and, at the particular urging of Defense Minister Ariel Sharon, decided on a large-scale military intervention to eliminate the Palestinian problem. Thus began the fifth Arab-Israeli war, called

Secretary of Defense Caspar Weinberger holds a press conference at Landing Zone One in Beirut during a visit to Lebanon in December 1982.

tinian camps. In the middle of July, the unlikely pair of pro-Soviet Syria and pro-American Saudi Arabia joined forces to suggest an evacuation of Palestinians under the protection of the United States. President Ronald Reagan agreed to use his best endeavors, and Special Envoy Philip Habib persuaded the sceptical Israelis to halt their advance so that the Palestinians could be evacuated, most to Tunisia in Greek ships, but some by road toward Syria.

The Marines Keep the Peace Once More

An American military presence was thus needed in Lebanon as part of a multinational effort, and the U.S. Marine Corps was again the force best placed to respond. Vice Admiral E.H. Martin's 6th Fleet had already landed one unit, part of Lieutenant Colonel James Mead's 32nd Marine Amphibious Unit, the marine component of Captain M.R. France's Task Force 61, to cover the evacuation of American citizens from Juniyeh on June 23-24, 1982.

Then on August 24, Lieutenant Colonel H.L. Gerlach's Battalion Landing Team 2/8 (2nd Battalion of the 8th Marine Regiment) landed in Beirut to cooperate with a paratroop battalion of the French Foreign Legion. They held the city's port while an Italian unit supervised the road to Damascus for Palestinians moving into Syria. This multinational force guaranteed that some 14,000 Palestinian "fighters" left Beirut, 8,000 of them by sea and the other 6,000 by land. With their task completed, the marines reembarked on September 10, and the multinational force ceased to exist Throughout the operation, the marines had been armed only with small arms, leaving all their heavier weapons offshore so that no one could claim that U.S. military strength had been used to aid Israel, a long-term American ally.

Another Intervention Required

Just four days after the marines had

Operation "Peace for Galilee" by the Israelis. Starting on June 6, the Israeli army launched a major offensive into southern Lebanon with the intention of pushing the Palestinians back at least 25 miles to create a buffer zone between the Palestinians and Israel itself. The operation soon developed into a much larger offensive. The Palestinians fell back in total disarray, and the Israelis came up against the Syrians, decisively beating them on the ground after securing total air superiority. The Israelis pressed on toward the edge of Beirut, where the bulk of the Palestinians were now concentrated and trapped.

Seeing an opportunity to destroy the Palestine Liberation Organization once and for all, Begin and Sharon committed Israeli forces to an attack into Beirut, using heavy artillery and air bombardment to blast a path toward the Pales-

Right: The American involvement in the Lebanese disaster.

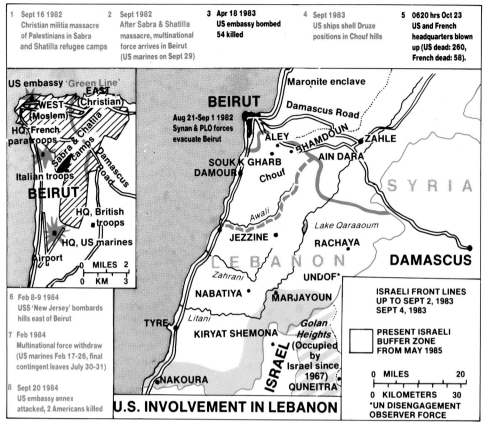

| 1 | Sept 16 1982 Christian militia massacre of Palestinians in Sabra and Shatilla refugee camps | 2 | Sept 1982 After Sabra & Shatilla massacre, multinational force arrives in Beirut (US marines on Sept 29) | 3 | Apr 18 1983 US embassy bombed 54 killed | 4 | Sept 1983 US ships shell Druze positions in Chouf hills | 5 | 0620 hrs Oct 23 US and French headquarters blown up (US dead: 260, French dead: 58). |

US embassy 'Green Line'
EAST (Christian)
WEST (Moslem)
HQ French paratroops
Italian troops
BEIRUT
HQ, British troops
HQ, US marines
Airport
MILES 2
KM 3

Sabra & Chatila Camps
Damascus Road

Maronite enclave
BEIRUT
Aug 21–Sep 1 1982
Synan & PLO forces evacuate Beirut
Damascus Road
ALEY
BHAMDOUN
ZAHLE
SOUK K GHARB
AIN DARA
DAMOUR
Chouf
SYRIA
Awali
Lake Qaraaoum
JEZZINE
RACHAYA
DAMASCUS
LEBANON
Zahrani
UNDOF*
NABATIYA
MARJAYOUN
Litani
TYRE
KIRYAT SHEMONA
Golan Heights (Occupied by Israel since 1967)
ISRAEL
NAKOURA
QUNEITRA

ISRAELI FRONT LINES UP TO SEPT 2, 1983 SEPT 4, 1983

PRESENT ISRAELI BUFFER ZONE FROM MAY 1985

0 MILES 20
0 KILOMETERS 30
*UN DISENGAGEMENT OBSERVER FORCE

6	Feb 8-9 1984 USS 'New Jersey' bombards hills east of Beirut
7	Feb 1984 Multinational force withdraw (US marines Feb 17-26, final contingent leaves July 30-31)
8	Sept 20 1984 US embassy annex attacked, 2 Americans killed

U.S. INVOLVEMENT IN LEBANON

Below: Armed with M16A1 assault rifles, U.S. Marines take cover behind a sandbag rampart during a terrorist attack on their position.

A marine of the American contingent in the multinational peacekeeping force in Beirut stands by the rear of a decidedly weary-looking M4 Sherman tank, a relic of World War II still used in limited numbers by a few of the world's smaller and less well-equipped armies.

reembarked, an agent of the Syrian government assassinated President Bashir Gemayel, and once again Lebanon appeared on the brink of unavoidable civil war. The Israelis moved into western Beirut to maintain civil order, but Lebanese Phalangists nonetheless managed to enter the Sabra and Shatilla camps and murder large numbers of the dependents left by the departed Palestinian "fighters": 460 people were killed including 15 women and 20 children. In an effort to stave off the inevitable, the new president, Amin Gemayel (brother of the murdered president) appealed for American and European assistance.

On September 20, President Reagan announced that the Multinational Peacekeeping Force was to be revived with American, French, Italian, and other forces. It would replace the Israeli and Phalangist forces maintaining order within Beirut until the Lebanese army could restore control.

On September 29, men of the 32nd Marine Amphibious Unit returned to Beirut. It was a period that was very uncomfortable for the marines, both

physically and emotionally. The marines held an enclave called "The Root" centered on Beirut International Airport, which extended inland from the coast as far as the Lebanese Scientific and Technical University. Inland from the Americans were the British, and the coast north of the marines (including the Bourj-al-Barajneh and Sabra/Shatilla camps) was held by the Italians. The French occupied western Beirut as far east as the so-called "Green Line" dividing the Christian and Islamic sectors of the Lebanese capital.

For the next year, the 32nd Marine Amphibious Unit (soon redesignated the 22nd Marine Amphibious Unit) alternated with Colonel Timothy J. Geraghty's 24th Marine Amphibious Unit as the American component of the Multinational Peacekeeping Force. Throughout the period of American involvement, there were incidents with the Israelis and the Lebanese militia forces, but they were generally very limited in nature, and the two units took only a few casualties. Between September 29 and October 30, the 22nd Marine Amphibious Unit

Opposite: A view of the U.S. Embassy in Beirut, which was destroyed by a terrorist bomb on April 18, 1983.

A somewhat incongruous sight: U.S. Marines caught in a traffic jam in downtown Beirut while patrolling in their M151 light vehicle.

suffered one killed and three wounded in action, from October 30 until February 15, 1983, the 24th Marine Amphibious unit had no casualties to its Battalion Landing Team 3/8 (the 3rd Battalion of the 8th Marine Regiment). Between February 15 and May 30, the 22nd Marine Amphibious Unit suffered seven wounded (two of them from non-operational causes) to its Battalion Landing Team 2/6 (the 2nd Battalion of the 6th Marine Regiment).

Bombing of the Marine Headquarters

The situation deteriorated sharply after the return of the 24th Marine Amphibious Unit to Beirut on May 30, 1983, when Battalion Landing Team 1/8 (the 1st Battalion of the 8th Marine Regiment) was the landed unit. A terrorist bomb destroyed the American Embassy in Beirut, and the marines were soon under sporadic artillery, mortar, and rocket fire It did little damage and inflicted few casualties, but it kept the men on edge the whole time. On the morning of October 23, however, a disaster overtook the unit; an unknown terrorist drove a truck laden with explosives into the battalion's headquarters building. The resulting explosion completely leveled the building, killing 245 marines and sailors, and injuring another 130. Even as the rescue of the wounded was taking place, replacements were flown out from Camp Lejeune in the form of Battalion Landing Team 2/6 (the 2nd Batallion of the 6th Marine Regiment), which remained until November 19 and suffered no casualties.

In its tour of duty up to November 19, therefore, the 24th Marine Amphibious Unit suffered casualties totaling 245 killed, 136 wounded in action, and four non-battle wounded. During much of this time, the American strength in

Captain, U.S. Marine Corps, Beirut (Lebanon), 1982

This officer is seen in the type of uniform that became standard for the marine units operating in Lebanon, where the greatest threat to their safety was presented by terrorists. The basic clothing is the "woodland" camouflage BDU (Battledress Uniform) made in a 50/50 mix of cotton and nylon for maximum protection against burns and colored with dyes treated to reduce their infrared signature. Over this the captain wears the vest of the PASGT (Personal Armor System, Ground Troops) system, which is a flak jacket made of bullet- and shrapnel-resistant Kevlar. The rank badge is pinned to the front of this flak jacket. The helmet is the venerable all-steel M1 in its last variant with LC-1 suspension and has a camouflage cover. The ALICE (All-purpose Lightweight Individual Combat Equipment) webbing seen here with minimal equipment, consists of a nylon belt and suspenders. The officer's weapons are the 0·45-inch (11·43-mm) caliber M1911A1 Colt automatic pistol and the 5·56-mm (0·22-inch) caliber M16A1 assault rifle. The latter is fitted with a rope sling and is attached to one of the suspenders, possibly as an anti-snatch measure.

Right: These Boeing Vertol CH-46 Sea Knights and a Sikorsky CH-53 Sea Stallion of the U.S. Marine Corps' air arm were parked close together at Beirut Airport and kept under constant guard against terrorist sabotage.

Below: An LCU (Landing Craft, Utility) prepares to leave the beach just south of Beirut after being loaded with equipment and vehicles on November 24, 1983.

As part of the multinational peacekeeping force in Lebanon, the 24th Marine Amphibious Unit kept up with its standard training schedule as far as possible. This camouflaged marine of the 24th MAU is participating in helicopter assault training.

Beirut had been boosted by Battalion Landing Team 1/3 (the 1st Battalion of the 3rd Marine Regiment), which served in Beirut between September 12 and October 10, but suffered no casualties.

The last tour of duty for the marines in Beirut started on November 19, 1983, when the 22nd Marine Amphibious Unit arrived after its detour for participation in ''Urgent Fury'' in Grenada. The unit landed its Battalion Landing Team 2/8 (the 2nd Battalion of the 8th Marine Regiment). By this time, it was clear that not only was the presence of the Multinational Peacekeeping Force yielding no real dividend; it was actually exacerbating the situation. U.S. involvement ended on February 26, 1984, when the 22nd Marine Amphibious Unit completed the American evacuation after a tour that had cost it 10 killed, one dead of wounds, and three wounded, as well as one non-battle death.

The Libyan Strike
(1986)

Thoughout the 1970s and 1980s, international terrorism continued to plague the world, and Americans abroad were among the choice targets for terrorists Much of the terrorism was attributable to political groups such as Italian, Japanese, and West German communist organiza-tions and nationalist groups such as the IRA, but the single most troublesome group was the Palestine Liberation Organization and its many splinter factions. These groups received support from a number of countries, including Syria, but during this period the country that seemed to offer Arab terrorists the greatest support was Libya, under the leadership of Colonel Muamar Ghaddafi.

The United States first came into conflict with Libya in the Mediterranean

Aviation maintenance men inspect the cockpit of a Vought A-7E Corsair III medium attack warplane on the flight deck of a U.S. Navy aircraft carrier during Operation ''El Dorado Canyon.''

Muamer Ghaddafi
For further references see pages 112, 115

during August 1981, though this occasion had nothing to do with terrorism. Contrary to international law, in 1973 Libya declared the extensive Gulf of Sidra, a 250-mile "bite" into the northern coast of Africa which included most of Libya's coastline, to be part of its territorial waters. As early as March 21, 1973, two Libyan fighters fired on a U.S. Air Force Lockheed EC-130 Hercules electronic reconnaissance airplane operating 83 miles from the Libyan coast, well beyond the 12-mile limit agreed under international law for territorial waters. Over the following six years, the Libyans ignored three U.S. "challenges" to Libyan ownership of these waters.

Further Trouble With Libya

On December 2, 1979, Ghaddafi allowed a Libyan mob to sack the U.S. Em-bassy in Tripoli, and the deterioration of Libyan relations with the United States became abundantly clear on September 16, 1980, when a pair of the Libyan air force's Mikoyan-Gurevich Mig-23 "Flog-ger" fighters unsuccessfully attacked a U.S. Air Force Boeing RC-135 surveillance plane, again well out over the part of the Gulf of Sidra claimed as international waters by the United States and its allies. President "Jimmy" Carter decided that there would be no response to these provocations, fearful that the Libyans might intervene with the Iranians and thus make the situation of the American hostages held in Tehran worse.

When he took office, President Ronald Reagan decided that the time had come to deal forcefully with Libya. He ordered that freedom of navigation exercises should be added into the framework of the 6th Fleet's operational training in the Mediterranean. As the Gulf of Sidra

Ordnancemen prepare to load an AIM-9 Sidewinder short-range air-to-air missile onto a Vought A-7E Corsair II medium attack warplane of the aircraft carrier U.S.S. *America* during Operation "El Dorado Canyon." This missile still has a protective cover over the transparency protecting the nose-mounted infrared seeker unit, and visible slightly above the missile is the Corsair II's retractable inflight refueling probe.

was an area where training was regularly undertaken, conflict with Libya seemed inevitable.

In August 1981, Vice Admiral W.H. Rowden's 6th Fleet formed Rear Admiral James E. Service's Task Force 60 for a scheduled training exercise. In this exercise, target drones would be tackled by air-to-air missiles launched from the aircraft of the air wings operating from the carriers U.S.S. *Nimitz* and U.S.S. *Forrestal*, and by the surface-to-air missiles fired by the escorting cruisers U.S.S. *Mississippi* and U.S.S. *Texas*. Notifications were issued to the relevant international bodies, including the Tripoli flight information region, and covered a large area whose southern tip protruded just south of the latitude line of 32° 30′ North which marked the northern edge of the sea area claimed by Libya.

As the exercise proceeded, Libyan aircraft undertook constant probes

against its southern edge, and the carrier pilots met more than 35 two-aircraft flights of Libyan aircraft; six of these flights entered the notified exercise zone. Then, on the night of August 18, Libyan television reported that American warships were approaching the Libyan coast and that Libyan forces had been put on full alert.

On August 19, several Libyan aircraft flew north, resulting in more meetings between American and Libyan aircraft. Then the commander of the VF-41 squadron from the *Nimitz* spotted two more intruders, and the sighting was confirmed by Commander Henry M. Kleeman's wingman in another Grumman F-14A Tomcat fighter.

The warships and the orbiting Grumman E-2 Hawkeye airborne early warning aircraft could not detect these aircraft on radar, so the Tomcats were ordered to investigate. What Kleeman and Lieutenant Lawrence M. Muczynski found was a pair of Sukhoi Su-22 "Fitter-J" attack aircraft. The two U.S. fighters closed the range as their crews tried to determine the intentions of the Libyan pilots, but then Kleeman saw the bright flare of a rocket motor as one of the Su-22s fired an AA-2 "Atoll" air-to-air msisile.

Two Libyan Aircraft Shot Down

A routine investigation now became a real engagement, and the American pilots had the advantages of superior equipment and better training. The result was a foregone conclusion: each of the Tomcats downed one Su-22.

The furore over this incident soon faded, but soon another incident with Libya occurred. It was an altogether larger affair, resulting directly from terrorism and having considerable long-term ramifications. The incident that sparked the episode was the terrorist hijacking of an Italian cruise liner, the *Achille Lauro*, by Palestinian terrorists on October 7, 1985. Before they ended the hijacking on October 9 by surrendering to the Egyptian authorities, the terrorists killed an American citizen, the wheelchair-bound Leon Klinghoffer, although his death was

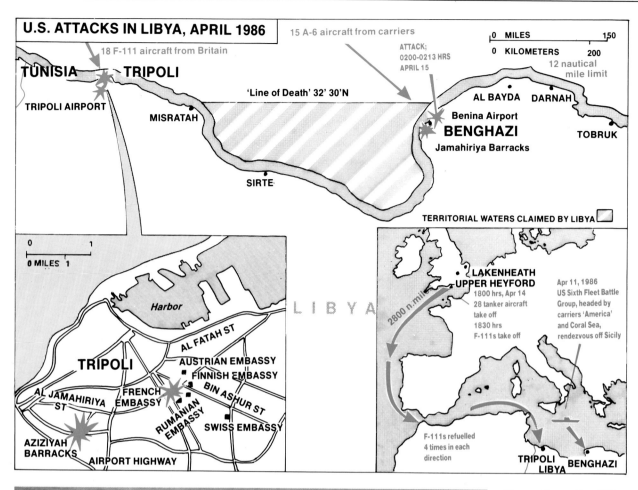

U.S. ATTACKS IN LIBYA, APRIL 1986

18 F-111 aircraft from Britain

15 A-6 aircraft from carriers

ATTACK;
0200-0213 HRS
APRIL 15

0 MILES 150

0 KILOMETERS 200

12 nautical mile limit

TUNISIA TRIPOLI

TRIPOLI AIRPORT

MISRATAH

'Line of Death' 32' 30'N

AL BAYDA DARNAH

Benina Airport

BENGHAZI

Jamahiriya Barracks

TOBRUK

SIRTE

TERRITORIAL WATERS CLAIMED BY LIBYA

0 MILES 1

Harbor

TRIPOLI

AL FATAH ST

AUSTRIAN EMBASSY

FINNISH EMBASSY

BIN ASHUR ST

AL JAMAHIRIYA ST

FRENCH EMBASSY

RUMANIAN EMBASSY

SWISS EMBASSY

AZIZIYAH BARRACKS

AIRPORT HIGHWAY

LIBYA

LAKENHEATH
UPPER HEYFORD

1800 hrs, Apr 14
28 tanker aircraft
take off
1830 hrs
F-111s take off

Apr 11, 1986
US Sixth Fleet Battle
Group, headed by
carriers 'America'
and Coral Sea,
rendezvous off Sicily

2800 n.mile

F-111s refuelled
4 times in each
direction

TRIPOLI
LIBYA

BENGHAZI

Above: Operation "El Dorado Canyon:" the U.S. strike against Libya.

Left: Visible in this one small area of the U.S.S. *America*'s flight deck during Operation "El Dorado Canyon" are four Grumman F-14A Tomcat fighters and one Grumman A-6E Intruder medium attack warplane.

reported only after the terrorists had left the ship to be taken eventually to Libya in an EgyptAir Boeing 737.

On October 13, American carrierborne aircraft intercepted the airliner in international airspace and forced the pilot to divert to Sigonella Naval Air Station in Sicily, where the Italians arrested six Palestinians. Four were sent to jail, but the two ringleaders escaped trial as they carried diplomatic passports.

Operation "El Dorado Canyon"

Ghaddafi was furious with the American and Italian part in this affair and commissioned the terrorist organization of Abu Nidal to extract revenge. There followed a series of outrages and American reactions. The bombing of a West Berlin discotheque on April 5, 1986, which killed an American serviceman and a Turkish woman, finally persuaded the U.S. government that only a major blow against Libya might halt the continued tit-for-tat series of terrorist actions and small-scale American responses. Thus was born Operation "El Dorado Canyon," a major but still limited air effort to destroy major parts of Libya's terrorist

framework and persuade Ghaddafi that, in the long run, he could not defeat the United States.

The targets were terrorist facilities in Tripoli and Benghazi, and Libyan air force targets such as Benina military airfield and the national air-defense radar network. U.S. forces involved in the operation, launched on April 14, were provided by the air force, the navy, and the marine corps. The air force used General Dynamics F-111F long-range interdictors of the 20th and 48th Tactical Fighter Wings, operating from British bases. The planes had the support of Strategic Air Command inflight refueling tankers for their long approach and departure flights, because they had been denied permission to overfly France and Spain. The navy and marine corps used the attack aircraft of Carrier Air Wings 1 and 13 from the U.S.S. *America* and U.S.S. *Coral Sea* of the 6th Fleet's Task Force 60.

One F-111 was lost from the attacking force of 18 F-111Fs, 15 Grumman A-6E Intruders, six Vought A-7E Corsair IIs, and six McDonnell Douglas F/A-18A Hornets, and the results are summarized in the accompanying chart. The raid caused considerable uproar around the world, but had the desired effect: it persuaded Ghaddafi to call off his terrorist campaign.

A Grumman F-14A Tomcat fighter, with its variable-geometry wings fully extended, lands on its carrier after a mission. The plane was part of the strength of VF-102 "Diamondbacks," one of the fighter squadrons forming Carrier Air Wing 1 embarked on the U.S.S. *America*.

Involvement in the Iran-Iraq War
(1988)

Marines disembark from an LCU (Landing Craft, Utility) into the surf of the Egyptian coast during a joint service exercise, "Bright Star '87," which took place in August 1987.

In 1980 Iraq launched a major war against Iran with the object of overthrowing certain provisions imposed on Iraq by the Treaty of Algiers in 1975. This treaty set the southern section of the frontier between the two countries as the halfway point of the Shatt-al-Arab waterway, through which the combined Tigris and Euphrates rivers emerge into the northern part of the Persian Gulf. The waterway was of vital strategic and commercial importance to Iraq, which felt that its interests were seriously threatened by Iranian imperialism. In 1971 Iran had indicated its expansionist desires by annexing the Musa, Greater Tunb, and Lesser Tunb islands on the western side of the Strait of Hormuz which connects the Persian Gulf with the Arabian Sea and the Indian Ocean.

Iran was clearly seeking to secure a strategic stranglehold on the region, but Iraq's smaller population and inferior armed forces forced it to play a waiting game. In 1979 the imperial dynasty of Shah Reza Pahlavi was overthrown by a fundamentalist Moslem revolution. Iraq launched its war against Iran the following year. It was a major risk, for Iraq was gambling on its belief that the revolution and subsequent turmoil had weakened the Iranian armed forces to the extent that Iraq could gain a swift victory.

Iraq had misread the situation and the temper of the Iranian people, who fought back with enormous determination. The mirage of swift victory was soon replaced by the specter of a long and bloody war, since neither side had the skills to secure

Left: The U.S. Navy maintains its 6th Fleet in the Mediterranean Sea as a powerful formation with modern warships. Here a Sikorsky SH-60B Seahawk helicopter undertakes antisubmarine operations for the battle group centered on the aircraft carrier U.S.S. *Saratoga*. In the background are the cruiser U.S.S. *Ticonderoga* and other, unidentified ships.

Below: men of the U.S. Marine Corps take up their positions for an attack during the amphibious assault phase of Exercise "Bright Star '87" at El Hamman in Egypt.

THE MILITARY HISTORY OF THE UNITED STATES

Above:
Recommissioned
under the American
flag, a line of laden
Kuwaiti oil tankers
proceeds down the
Persian Gulf during
September 1987 under
escort by a U.S. Navy
detachment including
an aircraft carrier.

Right: Adapted by the
Iranians as a
command and control
position for their light
forces, this oil platform
was set ablaze by
gunfire from U.S. Navy
destroyers on October
19, 1987.

overall superiority. Iraq's forces generally had superior weapons and greater tactical skills, but they were balanced by Iran's larger population and, effective, often suicidal, resistance. So the war settled down to an apparently endless campaign of bloody attrition in which neither side could gain the upper hand.

Given the stalemate on land, both countries looked to alternative methods of striking at the enemy. The air offered possibilities, but Iran's air force was too small, and it lacked spare parts to carry out a sustained offensive. Iraq, on the other hand, had an air force with better equipment and training, which made attacks on Iran's oil installations and, when provoked, on Iranian cities. This aerial campaign began early in the war with mutual attacks on each other's oil installations, but then settled down to occasional Iraqi attacks, sometimes on Iranian cities, but more often against offshore oil installations and "large naval targets" (the Iraqi euphemism for the tankers sailing down the Gulf loaded with

Iranian oil for export) Iran's counterattacks, limited by the country's lack of an effective air force, generally used missiles (typically the Soviet-supplied "Scud") against area targets such as cities. In 1987 Iran began to receive useful numbers of Chinese HY-2 "Silkworm" surface-launched antiship missiles, which were used in limited numbers against the oil installations of Iraq's Arab neighbors to the south, notably Kuwait and Saudi Arabia.

Neither side had a navy large or powerful enough to make formal naval war possible. The Iranians managed to bottle up the Iraqi navy in Umm Qasr, so the naval campaign descended to the level of hit-and-run attacks. Most of these raids were made by the Iranians, whose Revolutionary Guard Corps enjoyed virtual autonomy from the rest of the armed forces to operate from forward bases in the Gulf ports and islands with speedboats. Attacks were usually launched with rockets and small arms against tankers with rockets and small arms. The Iranian

A Sikorsky RH-53D Sea Stallion mine countermeasures helicopter of the U.S. Navy's HM-14 squadron goes about its business in the Persian Gulf in October 1987. The frame between the partially open rear door and the tail boom was used to tow a minesweeping sled that could be optimized for clearing acoustic-, magnetic- and pressure-activated mines.

The obsolete Mk33 open mounting for two 3-inch (76-mm) antiaircraft guns identifies the parent vessel as one of the navy's older amphibious warfare vessels, the U.S.S. *Mount Vernon*, an LSD (Landing Ship, Dock) of the five-strong "Anchorage" class built in the late 1960s and early 1970s. Operating in the Persian Gulf during October 1987, the ship is seen against a watery backdrop that includes a Sikorsky SH-3 Sea King helicopter of HC-2 (Helicopter Combat Support Squadron 2).

This photograph typifies U.S. operations in the Persian Gulf during 1987. Here a plane director signals directions to the pilot of a Sikorsky SH-60B Seahawk helicopter from Detachment 2, HSL-45 (Helicopter Light Anti-Submarine Squadron 45), as the machine is refueled aboard the guided-missile frigate U.S.S. *Ford*. This "Oliver Hazard Perry" class ship was involved in the escort of reflagged tankers.

Two electronics technicians man a 25-mm Chain Gun cannon during target practice aboard the "Oliver Hazard Perry" class guided-missile frigate U.S.S. *Nicholas* during service in the Persian Gulf. Weapons of this type were added to the frigates for the destruction of floating mines and Iranian light craft that might try to attack on suicide missions.

The guided-missile cruiser U.S.S. *England* lies at anchor in the Persian Gulf in January 1989. The ship is the seventh of the nine ''Leahy'' class cruisers, which have two twin-arm launchers for Standard surface-to-air missiles as their primary weapons for the protection of carrier battle groups. Tied alongside the *England* is a barge to allow smaller craft, such as that on the right, to visit the cruiser.

effort was very difficult to counter and resulted in substantial losses and damage to the world's tanker fleets. The Revolutionary Guard Corps also attempted a number of small minelaying offensives.

In 1987, these combined speedboat and mine offensives prompted an international effort, spearheaded by the U.S. Navy, to protect the tanker trade in the Gulf. There were several clashes, the most serious being an attack on the frigate U.S.S. *Stark* in March 1987 by an Iraqi air force Dassault-Breguet Mirage F1, whose pilot mistook the American warship for an Iranian target. The Iraqi pilot fired two French-supplied Exocet antiship missiles, which both hit the *Stark*, causing severe damage and killing 37 American personnel. Most of the other clashes took place between U.S. naval forces and the Iranians, who almost invariably lost. However, the particular state of mind that

made the Iranian version of Islamic fundamentalism so dangerous to a foe, also made it impervious to the logical conclusion that an armed confrontation between Iranian and American forces would almost surely result in military victory for the United States. The U.S. Navy later rode convoy on tankers reflagged under American colors as far north as Kuwait, while an international force of British, French, Italian, Belgian, and Dutch warships operated in the southern reaches of the Gulf, largely for mineclearing operations.

Eventually the scale of the Iranian effort dwindled as American warships and support aircraft destroyed Iran's attack boats and the deserted oil platforms they used as operating bases. In 1990 the Iranians and Iraqis agreed to an armistice, which allowed the international naval effort for the Persian Gulf to be scaled down to its peacetime level.

Photographed in January 1989, crewmen stand ready at their stations on board
the ocean minesweeper U.S.S. *Fearless* during operations to keep the Persian Gulf clear
of mines and thus free for the movement of oil tankers. The *Fearless* is one of just 19
survivors from the very similar ''Agile'' and ''Aggressive'' minesweeper classes, 58
ships built as a result of the U.S. Navy's experiences in the Korean War.

The Invasion of Panama
(1989)

From 1945 a fundamental shift in the relationship between the United States and its protectorate, Panama, began to emerge. A distrust of American political motivations and policies gradually evolved alongside a continuing admiration for American goods and culture. Succeeding U.S. administrations were caught between recognizing the validity of Panamanian aspirations for greater national sovereignty, but also wanting to preserve American control over the Panama Canal. Lyndon B. Johnson saw that a fundamental change in American-Panamanian relations was inevitable, but, like his successors up to President Carter, he was deterred by the difficulties that

such a change would entail. There were 13 years of intense and often heated discussions before the 1977 Torrijos/Carter Treaty, which rescinded the Hay/Bunau-Varilla Treaty of 1903 and provided for control of the Panama Canal to pass in specific stages to Panama until the United States relinquished its ownership at the end of 1999.

After 1977, the three major objectives of American relations with Panama were supposedly the protection of American lives in Panama, the enforcement of the various provisions of the Panama Canal treaty, and the maintenance of the democratic process in Panama. A fourth objective, added later and ultimately the objective that spurred the invasion in 1989, was the bringing to justice of General Manuel Antonio Noriega. He had become leader of Panama in 1983 after the death in 1981 of General Omar Torrijos in an air crash, and in the earlier part of his career, he had established close and useful ties with the

Aerial fire support for the American force involved in Operation ''Just Cause'' was provided by Lockheed AC-130 ''Spectre'' gunships converted from C-130 Hercules transports. Seen on the port side of this plane are the muzzles of a 105-mm (4·12-in) howitzer and 40-mm Bofors gun, separated by the bubble fairing that covers specialized electronic targeting equipment.

Private, 82nd Airborne Division, U.S. Army, Panama, 1989

Wearing the lightweight BDU (Battledress Uniform), improved paratrooper's combat boots, a flak jacket, and ALICE (All-purpose Lightweight Individual Combat Equipment) nylon webbing, this trooper of an infantry regiment (airborne) of the 82nd Airborne Division sports a Kevlar helmet developed as part of the PASGT (Personal Armor System, Ground Troops) kit. The first formation to receive this so-called "Fritz" helmet was the 82nd Airborne Division, some of whose units were issued with the helmet's paratrooper version (with different internal suspension) in 1983 just before the Grenada operation. The American flag and white tape were worn for identification purposes; the weapon is the 5·56-mm (0·22-inch) caliber M16A1 assault rifle.

Left: Operation "Just Cause" attracted enormous media attention. Here, the invasion's operational commander, Lieutenant General Carl W. Stiner, answers questions from a radio reporter.

Below: Smoke pours from the ruins of the Panamanian Defense Force's headquarters as an American helicopter maintains an aerial watch over Panama City.

Manuel Noriega

For further references
see pages
124, 128, 131

United States. More recently, however, the enigmatic Noriega had become known as a ruthless political operator. He killed his opponents and had also become an active participant in drug-running operations between South America and the United States.

Relations between the United States and Panama declined steadily from June 1987 throughout 1989. The final straw came on December 16, 1989, when Marine 1st Lieutenant Robert Paz was shot and killed by members of the Panamanian Defense Forces as he drove past the Comandancia, Noriega's main military headquarters. The Panamanian authorities claimed that Paz was a threat to Noriega's security and therefore a legitimate target. This was manifestly untrue, and in Washington it was now felt that to do something, no matter what, about the situation in Panama was better than doing nothing. President George Bush therefore authorized the implementation of an invasion plan that had been under preparation for the last three months.

American Citizens in Panama

The Americans in Panama totaled 40,000 men, women, and children. The largest group were the 13,000 regular force personnel of the Southern Command, General Maxwell R. Thurman's Panama-based unitary command responsible for defending of American interests in Panama and the rest of Central America. Other major elements included 7,500 additional troops deployed into Panama since the June 1987 crisis in U.S.-Panamanian relations, 7,000 dependents of these military forces together

The American operation resulted in widespread looting throughout Panama City as local citizens took advantage of the state of chaos.

Many of the Panamanian Defense Force's men changed into civilian clothes in an effort to evade capture, but large numbers were nonetheless detected and seized.

with personnel and dependents of U.S. civilian government agencies operating in Panama, 3,000 Americans still working on the Panama Canal and their dependents, and 10,000 other Americans working or retired in Panama.

None of these Americans ever felt threatened in a serious fashion by the Noriega regime or the 6,000 men of the Panamanian Defense Forces. There was also no real threat to the functioning of the Panama Canal as the U.S. implemented the gradually phasing-in of Panamanian personnel in preparation for the transfer of control to Panama at the end of the century. Panama had never had anything more than a nominally democratic government, so even this pretext for American intervention was lacking. Ultimately, therefore, the rationale for the American intervention was the need to bring Noriega to justice. In real terms, however, the most important need was to remove Noriega from office and thus strike a real blow at the drugs trade.

The invasion of Panama, codenamed Operation "Just Cause," was scheduled for December 20 by a force under the operational command of Lieutenant General Carl W. Stiner. A preliminary plan for the invasion of Panama had been prepared during the administration of President Ronald W. Reagan under the codename "Black Knight." Thurman had reworked this basic plan after the failure of a coup against Noriega in October 1989, so that a knock-out punch could be delivered quickly to remove the chances of bloody street fighting in Panama City.

Operation "Just Cause" Gathers Strength

In addition to small units such as the U.S. Navy's SEAL (Sea, Air, and Land) team from Little Creek, Virginia, Operation "Just Cause" involved three major units, Task Forces Bayonet, Atlantic, and Semper Fidelis.

Task Force Bayonet, drawn from the Southern Command strength already in Panama, was centered on Colonel Mike Snell's 193rd Infantry Brigade (5th Battalion, 87th Infantry Regiment and 1st Battalion, 508th Airborne Infantry Regiment with mechanized support from the 4th Battalion, 6th Infantry Regiment of the 5th Mechanized Infantry Division based at Fort Polk, Louisiana). This force was entrusted with isolating the Comandancia, the headquarters of the Panamanian Defense Forces, and securing Panama City.

Task Force Atlantic included 2,600 airborne troopers of a composite airborne brigade (units drawn from two brigades of the 82nd Airborne Division at Fort Bragg, North Carolina), 1,300 army rangers (drawn from the 1st, 2nd, and 3rd Battalions of the 75th Ranger Regiment based respectively at Fort Stewart and Fort Benning, Georgia, and Fort Lewis, Washington), and a backup force of conventional soldiers (2nd Brigade of the 7th Infantry Division based at Fort Ord, California). This task force's role was to take the Pacora River Bridge, capture Torrijos International Airport and the neighboring military air base at Tocumen, and seize Rio Hato, a Panamanian base about 90 miles southwest of Panama City.

Task Force Semper Fidelis, made up of 430 marines drawn from three marine corps units already in Panama (the Marine Corps Security Force Company at Rodman, Panama; Company "K" of the 3rd Battalion, 6th Marine Regiment, from Camp Lejeune, North Carolina; and a detachment of the Brigade Service Support Group, also from Camp Lejeune), was to seize the Bridge of the Americas over the Panama Canal. This action would cut off Panamanian forces in Panama City from any chance of reinforcement from the north and in the process secure Howard Air Force Base, the staging post for the overall operation. Another Panama-based marine composite unit, comprising the 1st Fleet Anti-Terrorist Security Team from Norfolk, Virginia, and Company ''D'' of the the 2nd Light Armored Infantry Battalion from Camp Lejeune, was entrusted with the neutralization of La Chorrera, a town where a strongly pro-Noriega garrison was located.

The U.S. Air Force provided support in the form of seven Lockheed AC-130H gunships of the 1st Special Operations Wing based at Hurlbut Field, Florida, together with an aerial reserve of two AC-130Es from Duke Airfield, Florida. It also included six Lockheed F-117A ''Stealth'' attack warplanes of the 4450th Tactical Group based at Tonopah Test Range Airfield on the huge complex at Nellis Air Force Base, Nevada; 26 units

of the Strategic Air Command's inflight-refueling tankers from 14 bases in the continental U.S.; 27 units of the Military Airlift Command's transports from 21 bases in the continental U.S.; and six units of the Military Airlift Command's communications support aircraft from six bases in the continental U.S.

No Emphasis on Tactical Air Power

In this considerable air strength, the virtually complete absence of tactical aircraft other than ''Spectre'' gunships and ''Stealth'' attack warplanes is noteworthy; of the latter, only two were used in the campaign. The reason was the desire to minimize civilian casualties in the fighting, which would inevitably be centered on Panama City. For the same reason, it was decided to keep artillery fire to a minimum and to use it only when authorized by a major general. Accurate fire support was nonetheless essential, but it could be provided in large measure by the ''Spectres.'' Where such aerial

The LAV-25 (Light Armored Vehicle armed with a 25-mm cannon) performed very well in the hands of the U.S. Marine Corps.

firepower could not be brought to bear, ground-level support was necessary. Stiner arranged for eight McDonnell Douglas Helicopters AH-64A Apache battlefield helicopters to be ''smuggled'' into Howard Air Force Base before the invasion. With them were four M551 Sheridan light tanks, each carrying a 152-mm (6.1-in) main gun that could fire a conventional shell or a Shillelagh laser-guided projectile. Another eight Sheridans were paradropped from Lockheed C-141 StarLifter transports on the night of the invasion, but two were lost after their parachutes became entangled in midair.

Operation "Just Cause" is Launched

The invasion was launched at 9:00 p.m. on December 19 after a three-hour delay caused by an ice storm at Pope Air Force Base, the North Carolina departure point adjacent to Fort Bragg, assembly area for the airborne forces involved in Operation "Just Cause." Operations in and over Panama started early in the morning of December 20, with the intention of securing all-important objectives in a single, concentrated wave of attacks. The intensive phase of the invasion lasted only five hours; although the Panamanian Defense Forces offered greater resistance than had been anticipated, their main strength was soon eliminated. This left numerous pockets of minor yet harassing resistance, and during the following two days, additional forces were flown in from bases in the U.S. to raise American strength in Panama to more than 27,000.

The capture of the Comandancia resulted in the heaviest fighting of the operation, and after the loss of this key point, the resistance of the Panamanian Defense Forces faded rapidly. The young, inexperienced soldiers had initially fought with considerable determination, but they were soon deserted by their politically appointed officers. They lost their enthusiasm for sustained combat, and most of them sought to melt into the background after changing into civilian clothes. More than 5,000 suspected members of the Panamanian Defense Forces were captured or detained during Operation "Just Cause." The U.S. forces also captured immense stocks of weapons, many of Soviet origin: more than 52,000 weapons (including 10,000 AK-47 assault rifles in crates marked "surveying instruments"), over 600 tons of ammunition, and more than 35 tons of explosives were seized.

Only after the collapse of the Panamanian Defense Forces' organized resistance did any real threat to American civilians living in Panama emerge. It came from the "Dingbats," the disparagingly nicknamed members of Noriega's Dignity Battalions.

Created in 1988 as home-defense units, the Dignity Battalions contained more "low-life" elements and criminals than genuine patriots. The battalion was called up just as the invasion began, but crumbled at the same time as the Panamanian Defense Forces. It was an ideal opportunity for the battalions' armed but lawless elements to split into small groups and spread through Panama City to loot, snipe, and burn buildings. It was at this time that American civilians were most threatened, but the crisis soon passed. After some tense hours the safety of the three main groups of American civilians was secured.

Noriega Surrenders

The capture of Noriega was high on the list of American priorities, but the Panamanian leader proved most elusive. His whereabouts were finally located only on December 24, when he took refuge in the Vatican Embassy. For ten days, Noriega refused to move, but on January 3, 1990, the Panamanian leader surrendered to Major General Marc Sisneros, Thurman's deputy in the Southern Command. Bundled into a Sikorsky UH-60 Black Hawk helicopter and flown to Howard Air Force Base, he was arrested by agents of the Drug Enforcement Administration, loaded onto a Lockheed C-130 Hercules transport, and flown to Homestead Air Force Base, Florida, before being transferred to jail.

Thus Operation "Just Cause," one of the strangest American military operations of all time, ended. The invasion resulted in the deaths of 23 American service personnel, together with three civilians. Panamanian losses were initially estimated by the U.S. at 314 personnel of the Panamanian Defense Forces and 202 civilians, although the Department of Defense later revised these totals to about 50 and more than 1,000 respectively. Some Panamanian sources put the civilian death toll as high as 5,000. The wounded totaled 324 Americans and at least 3,000 Panamanians.

Glossary

Aircraft carrier: The type of warship that took over from the battleship as the world's most important type of ship during World War II. In essence, it is a floating airfield with provision for hangaring, maintaining, and operating a substantial number of aircraft.

Armored personnel carrier: A vehicle designed for the movement of troops on the battlefield; generally a tracked vehicle that provides the men on board with protection against small arms fire. The troops are generally carried in a compartment at the rear of the vehicle accessed, in the case of the American M113, by a powered rear ramp/door.

Artillery: An overall term for tube weapons that fire shells (filled with explosives or other agents) rather than solid bullets, and which are too large and complex for operation by a single man.

Battalion: A basic subdivision of the regiment, generally consisting of fewer than 1,000 men and commanded by a lieutenant colonel.

Bomber: An airplane designed to deliver free-fall bombs, and therefore a comparatively large type with greater range than the fighter; the type generally carries its offensive weapons in a lower-fuselage bomb bay and has defensive gun turrets to deal with enemy fighters.

Brigade: The basic subdivision of a division, generally containing two or more battalions commanded by a brigadier general.

Company: The basic subdivision of a battalion, generally less than 200 men and commanded by a captain; the cavalry equivalent is the troop.

Destroyer: A warship intermediate in size and capability between a frigate and a cruiser. One of any navy's "workhorse" vessels it combines affordability with high performance and the size to carry a useful sensor and weapons outfit.

Division: The smallest army formation, made up of two or more brigades and commanded by a major general; it is the basic organization designed for independent operation and therefore contains support elements (artillery, engineers, etc.) in addition to its infantry.

Formation: Any large body of troops organized with capability for operations independent of the rest of the army and therefore possessing, in addition to its organic infantry units, the full range of artillery, engineer, and support services. The smallest formation is generally the division.

Gun: One of the basic weapons of the artillery, a higher-velocity weapon with a comparatively long barrel designed for the direct engagement (firing at an elevation angle below 45°) of targets that can be seen through the weapon's sight.

Howitzer: One of the basic weapons of the artillery, a lower-velocity weapon with a comparatively short barrel, designed for the indirect engagement (firing at an elevation angle of more than 45°) of targets hidden from direct sight by some intervening feature.

Logistics: The science of planning and carrying out the movement of forces and their supplies.

Materiel: The overall term for equipment, stores, supplies, and spares.

Mine: An explosive device generally encased in metal or plastic and designed to destroy or incapacitate vehicles, or to kill or wound personnel. The two basic types of mine are the land mine, a comparatively small weapon which is generally buried in the ground, and the sea mine, a considerably larger weapon either laid on the bottom of shallow waters or, in deeper waters, floating just below the surface at the top of an anchored cable.

Mortar: A tube weapon of the light type, consisting of a barrel, supporting leg(s), and a baseplate. It can be broken down into sections and carried by hand and is designed to fire its bombs on a high trajectory that ends with an almost vertical descent on the target.

Recoilless rifle: An antitank (and antibunker) weapon that generates no recoil as it fires a rocket-powered projectile.

Regiment: A basic tactical unit, subordinate to the brigade, consisting of two or more battalions under the command of a colonel.

Strategy: The art of winning a campaign or war by major operations.

Tactics: The art of winning a battle through minor operations.

Unit: Any small body of troops not organized with a capability for operations independent of the rest of the army. It therefore does not possess in addition to its organic infantry units, the full range of artillery, engineer, and support services. The largest unit is the regimental combat team, generally known in other armies as the brigade.

Bibliography

Abel, Elie. *The Missile Crisis.*
(J. B. Lippincott, Philadelphia, 1966).

Adkin, Mark. *Urgent Fury: The Battle for Grenada.*
(Lexington Books, Lexington, MA, 1989).

Ambrose, Stephen E. *Ike's Spies: Eisenhower and the Espionage Establishment.*
(Doubleday & Co., Garden City, NY, 1981).
Good account of the many covert operations undertaken during Eisenhower's presidency.

Beckwith, Col. Charlie A. and Donald Knox. *Delta Force – The U.S. Counter-Terrorist Unit and the Iran Hostage Rescue Mission.*
(Harcourt Brace Jovanovich, New York, 1983).
The account of the elite Delta Force commander.

Beschloss, Michael R. *May-Day: Eisenhower, Krushchev and the U-2 Affair.*
(Harper & Row Publishers, New York, 1986).

Cate, Curtis. *The Ides of August: The Berlin Wall Crisis – 1961.*
(M. Evans & Co., New York, 1978).

Collier, Richard. *Bridge Across The Sky: The Berlin Blockade and Airlift 1948-1949.*
(McGraw-Hill, New York, 1978).

Davis, Brian C. *Ghaddafi, Terrorism, and the Origins of the U.S. Attack on Libya.*
(Frederick A. Praeger, New York, 1989).

Detzer, David. *The Brink: Cuban Missile Crisis 1962.*
(Thomas Y. Crowell, New York, 1979).

Johnson, Haynes, et. al *The Bay of Pigs: The Leaders' Story of Brigade 2506.*
(W. W. Norton & Co., New York, 1964).

O'Shaugnessy, Hugh. *Grenada: An Eyewitness Account of the U.S. Invasion and the Caribbean History that Provoked it.*
(Dodd, Mead & Co., New York, 1984).

Petit, Michael. *Peacekeepers at War: A Marine's Account of the Beriut Catastrophe.*
(Faber & Faber, Winchester, MA, 1986).

Ryan, Paul B. *The Iranian Rescue Mission: Why It Failed.*
(Naval Institute Press, Annapolis, MD, 1985).

Teslik, Kennan L. *America's Involvement in Lebanon: Innocents Abroad.*
(Routledge, Chapman & Hall, New York, 1988).

Tusa, John and Ann. *The Berlin Airlift.*
(Atheneum, New York, 1988).

Wilson, George C. *Supercarrier: An Inside Account of Life on the World's Most Powerful Ship, the USS Kennedy.*
(Macmillan, New York, 1986). An excellent account about the American aircraft carrier that launched the ill-fated bombing mission into Lebanon.

Wyden, Peter. *Bay of Pigs: The Untold Story.*
(Simon & Schuster, New York, 1979).

Index

Page numbers in *Italics* refer to illustration